personal magic

personal magic

*A Modern-Day
Book of Shadows
for Positive
Witches*

MARION WEINSTEIN

WEISER BOOKS

This edition first published in 2021 by Weiser Books, an imprint of

Red Wheel/Weiser, LLC
With offices at:
65 Parker Street, Suite 7
Newburyport, MA 01950
www.redwheelweiser.com

ISBN: 978-1-57863-719-5

Library of Congress Cataloging-in-Publication Data available upon request

Cover design by Kasandra Cook
Interior by Deborah Dutton
Typeset in Adobe Jenson Pro, Incognito, and Weiss Std

Printed in the United States of America
IBI

10 9 8 7 6 5 4 3 2 1

Book Blessing

By the One Power over all,
By Diana, Hecate, Selene, Kernunnos, and Pan,
And all my other Deities—
Working for and through this Book of Shadows,
This book reaches only those for whom it is intended,
This work can never be misused;
And for those who use it rightly,
For the Good of All,
And according to Free Will,
May all the Positive Magic and Positive Witchcraft of
    the Universe
Bring joy and power for good
That cannot be measured.
And so mote it be.

Dedication

For my mother, Sylvia Under Weinstein, who taught me about magic and always corrected my spelling.

CONTENTS

PREFACE

Once we met in secret, in the dark
And whispered our words into the wind.
Now the work is free once more
And open to those who seek it.
For this we give thanks.
Here is our secret:
The Power comes from within
Now
Always
Forever

—Marion Weinstein

One draws from the well
Without hindrance.
It is dependable.
Supreme good fortune.

—*The I Ching*
Bollingen Edition
Hexagram 48
Six at the top.

A Book of Shadows is not a book of laws or commandments. Everyone's shadows are different; this is the way one Witch works, and some others with her. If you wish to use any of these ideas and techniques in your own work, you are welcome to them. They are not secret anymore.

INTRODUCTION

"Marion, Marion! Get in here—fast!" My mother was calling. "There's a man on television with Merv Griffin who says he's a Witch."

I raced into her room. There, on my parents' new color television, sitting on the couch next to Merv, was a crisp Englishman, with an impeccable accent. It was Raymond Buckland, newly arrived from England.

"... no, we do not worship the devil," he was saying.

"But some Witches worship the devil, don't they?" asked Merv.

"Those," Dr. Buckland replied tersely, "are Satanists."

It was a Pagan epiphany for me. What was the year? Early 60s, I'm pretty sure. Long before I was on radio, when I was just out of college or still in it, still trying to graduate that last painful senior year, still trying to pass one science class. I had written and produced the Junior Show the year before: *The Girl From*

Salem. It was a musical, in the grand tradition of ersatz college musicals of the 30s by Rodgers and Hart, and George and Ira Gershwin, shows like *The Boys From Syracuse.* It was about a Witch who goes to college and tries to fit in—just like me.

By that time, I knew I was a Witch, but I wasn't exactly sure what it meant. I was concerned about the old devil connection.

This was all cleared up for me by Raymond and Merv, and all the millions of viewers watching right after the 11 o'clock news and just before sleep.

Years later at a Goddess Festival, Dr. Buckland and I met and autographed our books for each other.

Years later still, my mother, widowed and in her 80s, joined my coven.

I first wrote my Book of Shadows in 1979. It was much shorter then, and deliberately intended for a small audience. In contrast to my other writings about magic, I wanted my personal Witchcraft to remain somewhat secret—for other Witches only. A member of my coven teased me for conducting my own "private Witch hunt," in this case not to persecute Witches, but to isolate them as book customers. The original subtitle of this book was, "A Dianic Book of Shadows." Some confusion arose when "Dianic" took on the popular meaning of only Goddess-worshipping, women Witches. This totally surprised me because "Dianic" meant that my primary alignment was with the Goddess Diana. It still is. But this was not a serious problem. In 1986, responding to demand, I begrudgingly allowed the book a wider distribution. At that time I added more material, but all of the original information remains in *Personal Magic* today, unchanged.

In the outside world, however, a great deal has changed. Witchcraft has grown into a viable, recognized religion (well, maybe not yet everywhere, but in more places every day).

Admittedly, our religion is still misunderstood, but its reputation is clearing daily. Wiccan groups meet openly on campuses, and protesters rally in outraged response to inaccurate Hollywood movies depicting Witches as evil. Witches regularly surf and meet online where numerous Witchcraft, Goddess-worshiping, and Neo-Pagan groups have websites.

Popular New Age techniques, such as affirmation and visualization, strongly resemble traditional Witchcraft work. Modern channellers contact their ancient guides with virtually the same techniques as Craft spirit contact. The Goddess is alive and well in the presence of woman ministers and rabbis in more traditional religions, even though the people involved may not directly know about Her—yet. The emerging public understanding about women's rights, children's rights, and animals' rights expresses Witchcraft beliefs of the centuries. Every time someone recycles, Paganism and other Nature religions—whose primary tenet is reverence for the Earth—take a giant step forward.

In the years since I first wrote this book, I, too, have made changes in my Witchcraft work. I have added more Deities to my personal pantheon. I now encourage others to do the same. Research led me to surprising but deeply relevant areas of family systems psychology and quantum physics. Everything is linked. When I perform my comedy, far more people understand it; when I give lectures and public appearances, far fewer people ask me if I worship the devil or turn people into frogs.

The religion of Witchcraft itself has been changing. First of all, there are more Witches, as more and bigger Pagan conferences and festivals demonstrate. Also, more women are becoming Witches. Not too long ago, politically focused feminists discarded all religions, viewing them as the opiate of the masses. Now they are becoming increasingly aware of the personal empowerment to be found in Goddess spirituality, specifically in the Wiccan tradition. More gay men are turning to Witchcraft, finding deep resonance in Wiccan beliefs and spiritual acceptance in a religion that welcomes all and judges none. And more heterosexual men are also becoming Witches, embracing the male ideal of nurturing husband, consort, father, and child of Nature—rather than the culturally limiting role of macho super-Deity personified.

A problem for some traditional religions today, is that although the cultural climate is rapidly changing as people are changing, religious beliefs and practices are expected to remain the same. Because Celtic Witchcraft was hidden underground for so many years—roughly from the 13th century to the present—there has been a compelling desire to resurrect it somehow, full-blown and intact, so that we can all be the Witches we would have been if the terrible medieval persecutions had never happened. But if Witchcraft had remained in the mainstream, it would have evolved and changed, perhaps more than any other religious tradition could have. Ours is a Nature religion, and Nature is constantly changing. Therefore, Witchcraft has growth and adaptability built right into it. And yet it hasn't changed at all, not at the core.

A Book of Shadows represents a Witch's most personal practice. In the interest of flexibility, I have departed slightly from the traditional Book of Shadows format to provide suggested alternatives to help you find your own way. If there is one thing I've learned since I wrote the first version of this book, it's that Witchcraft is decidedly not an organized religion. It is inner-directed, not outer-instructed. I have tried to convey this concept here—even though I provide instruction. Instead of instruction, I would rather say *suggestion*.

In oldest times, a Book of Shadows was kept for joyful reasons—to pass the work on to others. Every Witch who could write had one. In the Middle Ages, during the nightmarish Burning Times, Books of Shadows served another function—to preserve the religion while countless Witches perished. Today, we are back to the original purpose—sharing the work with others.

I am happy to share with you this, my latest work, as I simultaneously urge you to explore your own.

Blessed Be your Path.

part one

Primary Work

CHAPTER 1

Belief and Perception

Welcome to my religion. This is what I believe: Our lives extend in long limitless paths, behind birth and after death, not to mention in other realms and dimensions. The lifetime in which we are now living is a choice. We have chosen to live our lives at this particular time, and this particular time is a turning point on our planet Earth; it is a time of immense change.

Those of us who have chosen to live now are here for a reason. We formed our reasons in other lifetimes, other dimensions. Now we are here, in an apparently limited sphere of existence, and we find ourselves trying to remember: *Why are we here? Why now?* Many of us feel we can almost remember; some of us are convinced we do remember. One clue: This is a millennium time. Oh, we know that it's not a millennium, exactly. Our culture stopped using accurate calendars after the "lost" civilizations of the Aztecs, the Druids, the builders of the pyramids and the stone circles. But most of the planet agrees that this is a definitely important millennium time, so it becomes that, by means of perception.

Perception creates reality. Reality is infinitely flexible and can be directed, controlled, and created by us. In fact, that's what's happening all the time without our being aware of it or paying attention to it. But at this time, in the West, on our planet, most people do not perceive this to be true. So, it's not true for them, because what's true is what we perceive to be true.

The philosophy of Witchcraft contains a choice to perceive things differently from the way most other people do. Most people do not seem to agree with the choice part, the perception part, or even the infinite lifetimes part. Most people seem to prefer a belief system that is rational and pragmatic and that guarantees reality being essentially *inflexible*, no matter how horrific or painful. This is, somehow, reassuring to most people. I do not mean to sound patronizing about this. Everyone's reasons are completely valid. Speaking in terms of Witchcraft, there is great power in agreement, in agreed perceptions of reality.

For the past 2,000 years (at least), the perceived agreement has been that the world is an inflexible reality, created by outside forces (or Force, or Deity), something bigger than we are, which may or may not still be in charge of everything—and which has to be placated, pleased, or at least understood. The most popular conceptions of this bigger Thing are that it could be scientific theory or it could be a God. And for people who do not believe in this—whose numbers are increasing every day—there is one main alternative belief. This alternative worldview appears to be disorganized, chaotic, and random. In this view, whatever determines our lives is essentially meaningless—the fall of the dice or the luck of the draw—

and we *can't* placate it, influence it, or even understand it at all.

Current Choices of a Popular World View

Something or Someone bigger than we are is making things happen in ways we can't understand.

Someone has initially set everything in motion and is now letting us play everything out.

All of us are essentially "lost in the stars," like the Kurt Weill song and finding meaning and solace by being brave about it, or at least, resigned and responsible.

There are variations on these three, of course, and there are myriad details of theory within them. But these seem to be just about the only choices available. When I was thirteen years old, I thought a lot about the meaning of life. Presented with the standard American, Judeo-Christian worldview, one day I suddenly thought: *What if they're all wrong? The rabbis, the priests, the ministers—all of them!* Then my perception came up against the popular alternative: The chaos, the scary lost-in-the-stars feeling—and it was terrifying in the most primal, bleak, meaningless, unimaginably empty, Black Hole, anti-matter, soul-wrenching kind of way. I sort of stared at the emptiness and perceived it, not knowing what else to do. I felt shaken to the core of my being. And this lasted *several days*. Then, not exactly knowing how or why, I chose not to believe in any of it. I'm sure that was the moment I became a Witch.

Or that was the moment I *remembered* being a Witch in another life or lives (because reincarnation is part of the

Witchcraft worldview). I've been piecing my personal reality together ever since. I have chosen a religion that gives me permission—no, *encourages* me—to do this. I didn't have a name for my belief system at first, just a list of goals: To feel good about reality, to be comforted, to help people, to transform things, to make things happen, and to feel at home with all that is considered mysterious.

I celebrate Halloween as my most sacred, most meaningful day. *How do you know you're a Witch?* people ask. Others nod knowingly and use the words "Wiccan" and "Wicca."

These words apparently mean "wise" in Old or Middle English or Pre-Norman Anglo-Saxon. But even the meaning of *Wicca* is up for redefinition and debate. Some contemporary Witches posit that the words mean "to bend," as in bending reality. I actually studied Anglo-Saxon in college, in depth. I can quote *Beowulf* in the original, and not too many people can say that these days. I can tell you, nobody today is 100 percent sure what all the words mean.

Today, Witchcraft is a reconstructionist religion.

Every culture has—and has always had—Witches, Shamans, Wizards, Magicians, Sorcerers, and Wise Women. These people alternately helped their community or were persecuted by it. More accurately—these people helped the native peoples' communities and were persecuted by "organized religions," which frequently took over, in vast political maneuvers that would put modem dictators to shame. I refer specifically to the harsh version of patriarchal, monotheistic, allegedly Christian religion that swept across Europe, starting in the 13th century. The events of the 13th, 14th, and 15th centuries, cumulatively known to

Witches as *The Burning Times*, were definitely barbaric, geno-cidal, and bearing no resemblance to the essence of true Christianity. Before that, in the part of the world known as the Fertile Crescent, native people practicing Goddess worship and Paganism suffered a similar fate. But somehow the Old Ways always remained—hidden, underground, lurking in the shadows.

Halloween, Friday the 13th, the Equinoxes and Solstices, friendly spirits, astrology, bonfires, wishing wells, fairies, imps, elves, and Witches—these are some of the more popular remnants of the Old Religion. The Witchcraft that I prac-tice is Celtic, based on traditions found in the British Isles, dating back to Neolithic times, and possibly influenced by older cultures such as Middle Dynasty Egyptian, Cretan, Mesopotamian, and Atlantean.

Here's what I *do not* believe: I do not believe in a devil, and I certainly do not worship one. The idea of devil worship was invented during the 14th century, influenced by the Crusades. Devils and demons have nothing to do with Witchcraft. Their worship became Satanism, or so-called "black magic," which is a creation based on Christianity, defined as the ultimate anti-Christian belief. As Alex Haley (the author of *Roots*) said, "History is written by the oppressors." The history of Witchcraft was written by the Witch hunters and inquisitors. This is recorded, verifiable fact, which somehow was not questioned by historians until now. We still have to rewrite dictionaries, encyclopedias, and most definitions. There's so much for a Witch to do!

Also, I do not call myself a "white Witch," and I'm upset when other people do so. They may be trying to sound enlightened and open-minded, because they know I'm not a bad Witch as in fairy tales, folklore, and the Land of Oz. But white is not good, and black is not bad: those definitions are outdated and biased. How about Positive and Negative? I define myself as a Positive Witch. But actually, all Witches are Positive—all *real* Witches.

I often make the distinction between Positive and Negative Magic. It's outrageously simple, and absolutely not subject to interpretation. Positive Magic is for the good of all. So is Positive Witchcraft. Negative Magic and Negative Witchcraft is either blatantly harmful, or just the tiniest bit manipulative. Positive work respects the free will of all and is for the good of all. Negative work is based on a belief that someone has to be pushed around—even for their "own good." Negative work can have all sorts of rationalizations to make it seem right. But it is never right. Positive work never has to prove anything. It always works, and it always harms none.

Anybody who tells you that Witchcraft is exactly like this, and means exactly that, is probably making it up. And basically, that's fine. That's what's so wonderful and liberating about an inner-directed theology. You can make it up too, by perceiving your reality as something you can change, work with, and transform. Just don't try to impose your views on anyone else. Positive Witchcraft does not proselytize, not even to other Witches.

This is my definition of magic: Magic is *transformation*, brought about by will and skill in accordance with natural law. Witchcraft is a religion that uses magic as other religions use prayer. Actually, magic is the great-grandparent of prayer. Magic is the directed process of transformation, used in conjunction with Natural law. There is no "supernatural," there is only the natural (or as I like to say in my lectures, the *superdupernatural*). The natural world has been much neglected as of late; its power and beauty are just being rediscovered now. And, oh yes, *we are all part of the natural world.* We're not separate from it. That separation idea came from Descartes, who was definitely not a Witch.

Here is how I believe mysteries are solved: *There is an invisible web of meaning that ties together all the seemingly unrelated events, ideas, and beings in life—and beyond.* We can work with the strands of this web and see the connections. We can understand the apparent reality that people are agreeing to perceive all around us, and work with that too—as part of the total picture. This does not mean we should give up on modern technology or our current culture; it means we can add our ideas to it, create a blend.

Witchcraft is holistic; it includes everything. Native peoples all over the Earth have agreed with much of this, and have celebrated many similar ideas in song and dance, prayers, chants, and legends.

Incidentally, the word *Pagan* simply means "of the country." In the Middle Ages, Pagans were the country folk who refused to convert to Christianity, and who clung to the old ways of the Goddess and God, still celebrated the folk holidays, and revered Nature. During the persecutions, Pagans were at risk, and had to go underground to avoid certain death. Neo-Pagans today, or just plain Pagans, are "of the country." We honor Nature above all else. All Witches are Pagans, but Pagans can be Witches or not, Druids or not, Eco-feminists or not—or just plain Pagans.

The Inner Bell

I frequently refer to that inner sense of truth and deep knowing which we all possess. Some people call it psychic power and consider it mysterious. Some call it intuition, usually ascribed to women. Others call it inner guidance or higher self. But every Witch knows when something "rings true"— or when it doesn't. Our oracles help us to reach this level of understanding, and some magicians also turn to the spirit world for information about it. I recommend that we simply listen. Soon enough the Inner Bell will be heard, and once we have heard it, we know exactly what it is. It's as simple as that.

Some of us say we chose to be born into this life at this time to help bring Witchcraft back, to help bring back the Goddess. We are here to help bring back the world view that allows Witchcraft to flourish and that allows everyone, even non-Witches, to benefit from magic.

So this is what I choose to perceive. Sometimes it can seem really difficult to hold onto this perception in the middle of the United States, in New York City, while picking up your laundry or hailing a taxi. Or you could do magic for your laundry (divine protection and cleanliness), for the taxi (perfect safety, perfect timing and spacing), and for everything else in your life. Witchcraft is alive and well. It is ancient and ongoing, historic and retranslatable, and it applies to right now.

CHAPTER 2

The Basics

The only law of Witchcraft is The Threefold Law:[1]
Everything you do comes back to you three times.

Earth Magic works threefold:
The Work is stated and performed in the World of Form.
It goes out into the Invisible World, and comes back to manifest in the World of Form.

All work is for the good of all only
And according to free will—
thus harming none.

One cannot be a Witch "part-time." By definition, Witchcraft is a way of life and permeates all of life. A Positive Witch lives by these principles all through every chosen Witchcraft lifetime, awake and asleep, in work, in deed, in thought, and in intent.

This means no cursing, no harming. This means no stated negatives, and all negatives taken *out of The Law* (The Law of Cause and Effect).

This does not mean to *deny* negatives or the Dark. We *acknowledge* it, use it positively, strip it of all negative power, transcend it, and turn it to good.

The Two Worlds

The two Worlds in which we live are: The World of Form and the Invisible Realm. In this case, the World of Form is manifest as our planet, Earth. The Invisible Realm includes everywhere else. The Witch's magic is accomplished with the conscious use of both Worlds. Our goal is to move and to *live* perfectly and easily between the Worlds—always.

Earth Magic

The magic of the Witch connects the Cosmic to the Earth. Witch magic is visible, tangible, and practical. But the overview is essential.

Thus, we work in linear time, using The Law of Cause and Effect. We work with linear time, knowing full well that time is not necessarily linear, but actually all at once. All time coexists, and it is *because* we are aware of this overview that we are able to see the future, and to work magic forward and backward in linear time.

We work with the World of Form, and in it our magic manifests to the five senses: touch, sight, hearing, smell, and taste. Our techniques also employ the five senses—even though we know full well that space is not defined by what we touch, see, hear, smell, or taste. We know that all space coexists, limited only by perception. With the overview, our perception is the sixth sense—Spirit, represented in the pentagram by the Circle, which encompasses All.

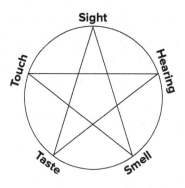

Words of Power

For Earth Magic, we use words, thoughts, images, ideas, and rituals to activate our work. We employ the basic, standard magical principles to connect the worlds. We follow the basic Words of Power technique:

1. There is One Power.

2. The Power includes All.

3. We are all perfect microcosms of the Power (thus we are linked to all beings).

4. Every being has Free Will and all work is for the good of All.

5. As microcosms of the One Power that includes All, we draw upon whichever aspect of the Infinite Power we wish to use, for whatever goals we state.

6. We affirm that the work goes out into The Law of Cause and Effect, and that it is done.

We follow this sequence of ideas, with one important difference: the use of *Alignments*. An Alignment is the direct connection that can be drawn between Deity and Witch. This powerful link, in effect, combines steps 2, 3, and 5 from the list.

Blessings, spells, and chants are based upon Words of Power.[2]

The Power of Words

As Witches, we believe that all of our words come true, not only when we are specifically working magic, but throughout all of our lives. We also believe that everyone, including every non-Witch, is continuously creating life experiences by means of the words that are spoken. So we may use the following antidotes if we ever hear negative words spoken by anyone—even ourselves:

+ I take that out of the Law (meaning the Law of Cause and Effect).

+ No harmful power, turn it to good.

+ Goddess (and/or God) forbid.

+ This is dissolved, released, and turned to good.

CHAPTER 3

Alignments
and Deities

The purpose of drawing Alignments is to identify ourselves so thoroughly with whatever aspect of the Power we have chosen (specifically aspects of the Goddess and the God), that we do not have to delineate Words of Power step-by-step. We can "ask" our Deities for use of Their Power—because we have already made that Power our own and earned it.

Of course, if we have not earned it, it does not come through to us.

Further, because we have chosen our Deities carefully, we trust Them, knowing that we are actually trusting ourselves as Their Incarnate Forms on Earth. In this context, asking a Deity for something is actually an affirmation.

We do not specify *forms* for the manifestation of our work. We allow the *essence* of whatever we are working for to reveal itself to us in perfect form. If we feel it's appropriate to name a form, we always add: "its equivalent or better."

This is not praying. It is not supplication. It is affirmation and trust of the microcosm/macrocosm. It is taking pure, personal responsibility without blame or guilt.

Guidelines

Ideas and *beliefs* exist in the Invisible World and they manifest in the World of Form. Magic is used to shape, control, and direct these ideas and beliefs and their consequent forms and manifestations.

Alignments connect us with the Goddess and the God. They define us as microcosms of the One Power.

Here is an example of a Deity Alignment:

I am Goddess Incarnate, perfectly Aligned with The God.

More detailed Alignments will follow.

Affinities are the consciously chosen connections between ideas and their manifestations in our lives. Affinities are pathways for magic.

Here are some examples of Affinities:

+ "When I perceive the love that exists all around me, I then manifest more love in my life."

+ "As I give thanks for the good that I already have, I then manifest further good in my life."

+ "I am a Positive Witch, so my life is filled with magic."

Form Contingencies are the opposite of Affinities. Form Contingencies are limited beliefs, which manifest in limited ways.

Here are some examples of Form Contingencies:

+ "If I have this, I cannot have that."

+ "If I am this, I cannot succeed as that."

+ "It don't mean a thing if it ain't got that swing."

Often Form Contingencies can be hidden beneath the conscious level and, consequently, may seem out of our control. But this is an illusion. It also can become difficult to locate them if we attach blame or guilt to having them in the first place. Their presence must be eliminated in order to fully practice Positive Magic. *Personal responsibility* is the key.

Guilt is blame of the self, and blame is guilt projected toward another. In order to go forward into the work, both must be stripped of all power and released.

No Guilt, No Blame!

Some Form Contingencies may be cultural, some karmic, and some a result of linear time conditioning—specifically from early experiences in this lifetime.

It is helpful to hold onto the *Overview*, which sees all of your lifetimes as one long life, demarcated by (linear) births, deaths, and rebirths. In such a widened context, Form Contingencies will automatically lose their apparent power.

Many Witches may still have a *persecution* Form Contingency attached to being a Witch. They may find themselves victimized in areas of life that may seem unrelated to Witchcraft. If this is the case, work to release this problem, and to replace it with the chosen Affinity that says being a Witch is a positive and powerful way to live. Let us joyfully remember that being a Witch means to live between The Worlds and to practice magic (Positive, of course) not only for oneself, but also to help others.

Power Sources and Deities

Our source of Power is the Moon, specifically in Her Three Goddess aspects of Diana, Selene, and Hecate.

+ Diana represents the Waxing Moon, the nurturer.

+ Selene represents the Full Moon, carrying the Infinity of Solution.

+ Hecate represents the Waning Moon, the dispenser of all Justice.

Our complimentary Power source is the Sun, specifically in the two Horned God aspects of Kernunnos the Consort, and Pan the Changeable.

Kernunnos lends balance, fire, and light. He is the Lover who blesses and guides sexual pleasure.

Pan shapes flexibility in the World of Form. He is the performer who watches over wit and entertainment.

Thus the five aspects of Deity with which we can work are points in the pentagram:

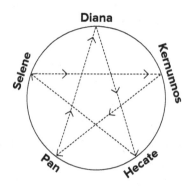

Note: The sequence in which you connect the points is, of course, up to your own discretion.

Deities

Since earliest times on this planet, people have related to Deities—Goddesses and Gods—as a focus for spiritual feelings. Specific visions of Deity are determined by personal emotional development as well as by the contemporary social and psychological climate. In rigid, structured cultures, there has never been room for people to choose their own Deities, nor even to interpret the ones provided for them. Yet Deities *are* a choice. This is something we may not realize because our culture has provided traditional images of Deity for us (white, male, paternal, all-powerful, all-good, and all-knowing).

As Witches, we know that Deities have always been a source of psychic power. Pressuring a group of people to change their beliefs and allegiance from one Deity or several to another—no matter how altruistic or enlightened the motives for such "conversion" may appear to be—is basically a technique to control people. The clergy may not directly control the new converts, but the society which the clergy represents will inevitably do so, with considerable financial gain. This has happened with all native peoples who were forced to relinquish—along with their Deities and their homeland resources—control of their entire lives.

In so-called holy wars, one culture's Deity is believed to vanquish another's. Unspeakable atrocities have been conducted in the name of religion, justified by the convenient depiction of a particular Deity as warlike. To reinforce this vision, destructive acts of nature are often interpreted as expressions of the Deity's wrath.

In most religions, questioning the Deity's power is considered a sin. Punishment can be psychological (such as ostracism and excommunication)—or much worse (prison, torture, and death). Today, in many parts of the world, it is, thankfully, no longer dangerous to question the character or even the existence of, Deity. In other times, it would have been an unfathomable luxury to say this, but one of my main recommendations has always been: *Create your own theology.* You can pick and choose from a vast array of spiritual traditions, or you can come back to the one you originally learned in this lifetime, but this time by *choice.* Or you can totally create every detail of your own personal religion.

I have never understood how people living in a free society, who felt disenfranchised from their birth religion, could—with relatively little exploration or research— jump right into another religious tradition, adopting all of its concepts and rules without question. This could be a relatively safe conversion into a mainstream religion, or worse, a dangerous conversion into a bizarre cult. I am not talking here about *thoughtful* religious choices, but thoughtless ones.

Thanks to my recent research in psychology, I have an explanation for this behavior: People are taught about religion in earliest childhood, when an unquestioning attitude and desire to please is the child's approach to learning from authority figures. This same attitude is later, unknowingly, carried into adult life. The child's vantage point also determines conceptualization of the Deity's character and people's relationship to it.

Small wonder that the Deity is most often conceptualized as parental in nature, specifically the kind of authoritarian parent who doesn't like questions.

As adults, our approach to religion should be filled with questions, and we should expect our Deities to provide answers that are deeply meaningful to us. We should keep exploring and creating until we are totally satisfied with our personal visions of our Deities. They should provide solace, inspiration, and guidance in our lives—and *the process should be ongoing*—as we ourselves grow and develop.

The entire history of Witchcraft is a history of persecution based on visions of Deity. Political proponents of patriarchal monotheism redefined Witchcraft's God as a "devil," and then persecuted Witches in the name of their own distorted Judea-Christian Deity. The Goddesses and Gods of Witches and Pagans have always been based on nature; they are believed to exist *within* all life forms without duality or hierarchy, rather than be separate or somehow "above" the natural world. This concept is called *immanence*. Indigenous religions all over the planet have always followed this belief, which is a totally different concept than a patriarchal monotheistic vision of external Deity.

The Dangers of Hierarchy

A hierarchal concept of Deity and clergy leaves plenty of room for self-styled authorities to interpret for the masses what the Deity "wants." This often includes unquestioning obedience and donations of money, both of which have to be given to the Deity's earthly representatives. The point is that when hierarchy is part of religious belief, there is room for manipulation. When hierarchy is considered valid, a system is already in place to make it possible and even plausible for a clergyman to claim that he speaks for the Deity, and that the Deity gave him personal instructions, so therefore others should listen to whatever he says. In the case of some charlatan clergy, this is the rationale for asking people to send money directly to them. In the case of the politically motivated, this is the rationale for encouraging persecution and war. In the case of sexual predators, the role of clergyman has (until recently) provided carte blanche for the shocking abuse of women and children. However, if the Deity is believed to deal with everyone directly and equally—none of these problems could ever happen.

So Deity is a choice—one of the most important choices a person can make. I will provide you with some of my choices, but the last thing I want is for you to embrace these Goddesses and Gods without thinking about how—or even whether—you relate to Them personally. So I have added a list of other possibilities for you, and urge you to meditate and conduct further research on your own. Diverse cultures on our planet have detailed a rich history of Deities, far beyond the ones listed here. This is just a beginning.

I have included a broad definition of ethnic origins. But please remember that when you choose your Deities, personal feelings of affinity and resonance are more important than your own ancestral roots in this lifetime. The reasons being, who knows what nationality you might have been, in alternate or former lives? Or want to be in future lives? For example, you might be a person of African heritage, yet feel drawn to Celtic and Greek Deities—or vice versa.

Also, please bear in mind, especially if you choose to do future research, that history has not been kind or accurate in the case of many Deities, specifically the Goddesses. Each successive religious perspective has had an agenda, aimed at denigrating the previous theology. As a general rule, recent feminist researchers have been able to transcend this cultural bias. For example, the Roman Goddess Juno has been popularly depicted as "wife of Jupiter." Her original status went far beyond that, as a powerful Mother/Creatrix Deity. Ishtar, whose original title of "Queen of Heaven" was denigrated by subsequent chroniclers to "Whore of Babylon."

So, the best way to provide the ultimate, inner-directed basis for your Deity choices is to meditate on the Deities that interest you. As you Align with your Deities, please remember: This process is a commitment to embody Their most powerful, inspiring qualities in your own life. Deities reflect directly into Their culture, and the culture projects its vision of itself onto its Deities. For example, a vision of a white, male God empowers the young, white boys of that culture. And who are the government leaders of such a society? Look around you. Visions of judgmental, warlike, punishing/rewarding Deities can condone family conflicts and international wars. A powerful Mother Goddess empowers girls and women. Does the Goddess influence a society even if She isn't yet a primary Deity? I believe this is happening right now, even amongst people who are unaware of the reemergence.

The Power of Capitals

Speaking of the Goddess, for far too many centuries a biased message has been sent out through capitalizing the word "God," as well as accompanying pronouns, *Him, His, He*—in all literature, including secular—while assigning lowercase references to all other Deities, notably the Goddess. Witches categorically capitalize the Goddess, including pronoun references of *Her, Hers,* and *She.* Why then, have I chosen to capitalize all references to Deities including God, including even Them? Because I do not wish to fall prey to the evils of lowercase gender bashing! All Deities deserve to be capitalized, whether we believe in Them or not. I am an equal opportunity gender chronicler of the sacred. That is only fair.

What are Deities?

Are Deities real? Did we create Them? Or did They create us? Are They inside us, or up in some heavenly sphere? Or all around us? Or all of the above? I leave this up to you. The process of aligning with, working with, and defining your own Deities is infinitely empowering. No one can do this for you, or tell you how to do it. But I'll give you a hint: The *feelings* the Deities evoke have the power—and the feelings are already within you.

My Personal Deities

Diana (Roman).
Selene (Greek).
Hecate (Turkish and Greek), Hekate.
Kernunnos (Celtic), Cemunnos.
Pan (Greek and Roman and throughout Europe).

Here are just a few examples of the rich Deities for you to contemplate, research, and choose:

Additional Goddesses

Artemis (*Greek*)—Goddess of healing, the Moon, wild animals, and physical strength in women. The twin of APOLLO. Greek version of DIANA.

Ceres (*Roman*)—Goddess of the grains, the harvest, and the Earth. Also, founder of the legal system, the Great Mother Nurturer. Women pray to Her when they want to have children.

Hestia (*Greek*)—First of all Divinities to be involved in all prayers. Essentially the same Goddess as Vesta (*Roman*), aspect of HESTIA (*Greek*) as seen previously—Goddess of the hearth and safe spaces. Her altar was the most sacred space in Rome and Her flame never went out. Her priestesses were called Vestal Virgins. At the time, virginity meant independence, not chastity.

Athena (*Greek*)—Goddess of wisdom. Warrior Goddess. Her temple was the Parthenon.

Yemenya (*African*) (Other spellings: YEMAYA, INMANJA)—Originally from Africa, also Brazilian. Holy Queen of the Sea. Has dominion over the Summer Solstice, and protects boats.

Morrigan (*Celtic*)—A triple Goddess. Mainly referred to as "THE MORRIGAN." Courageous, shapeshifter, sometimes associated with the Other World (after death).

Gaia (*Greek*)—Mother Nature. The Goddess of the planet Earth. Now Her name has come up again in the environmental movement, to tell us that the Earth is sacred and that we are all part of one being.

Isis (*Egyptian*)—Also known as Hathor Isis, Her milk was believed to have created the Milky Way. She ruled invention, law, agriculture, and was known for magic words. I have used Her term *Words of Power* for my work.

Nut (*Egyptian*)—Sky Goddess, ruler of night, the subconscious (dreams), and the stars.

Juno (*Roman*)—Queen of Heaven, Mother of The Goddesses and Gods, and numerous other titles. She ruled most areas of life and watched over all women.

Hera (*Greek* name of JUNO).

Devi (*East Indian*)—An all-encompassing Indian Goddess, She was said to hold the Guna strands of existence that make us see things as so-called "reality." This has a modern counterpart in atomic particles.

Ix Chel (*Mexican*)—Goddess of birth and the Moon.

Ishtar (*Near Eastern*)—Goddess of love, of prophetic visions, oracles, and prophecy; Goddess of all nourishment; Her title, "Queen of Heaven," was one of many praise-filled titles.

Rhiannon (*Celtic*)—Goddess of the Other World, birds are sacred to Her, specifically the raven.

Cerridwen (*Celtic*)—Goddess of the Cauldron, birth, and rebirth. The Birch is Her sacred tree.

Awehal (*Iroquois*)—Goddess who created the Earth, seeds, and animals.

Mawu (*Native American*)—She is said to have put a little piece of Herself (Sekpoli) in each person.

Nammu/Nina (*Near Eastern*)—The oldest Goddess name in recorded history. The Mother of all Deities.

Spider Woman (*Native American*)—The Creatrix of the peoples of the Desert Circle: Southwest United States and North Mexico, She wove existence—all the world—out of the Sun's rays. Also called SPIDER GRANDMOTHER.

Guadelupe (*Mexican, Aztec*)—A Brown Goddess and still a principal Deity in Mexico, She stands between the Moon and Sun's rays; Her cloak is covered with stars. In the 16th century, she became the "Patron Saint of the Western Hemisphere."

Oya (*African, Yoruba*)—Ruler of wind, fire, and thunder—and female power. The female Warrior Goddess, also healer and transformer.

Additional Gods

Neptune (*Roman*)—God of the Sea, ruler of dreams and visions. The planet is named after Him.

Posseidon (*Greek*)—Aspect of NEPTUNE (see above).

Osiris (*Egyptian*)—Consort/Husband to Isis. Rules the underworld and redefines death. Known for His miraculous regenerative capabilities. His symbol is the Ankh.

Apollo (*Greek*)—Twin to Artemis. God of the Sun, music, and medicine.

Hermes (*Greek*), **Mercury** (*Roman*)—Messenger God. God of communication.

Ra (*Egyptian*)—Sun God, parent of all the Gods and Goddesses.

Chae Noh Ek (*Mexican*)—Brother/Lover of the sun star Venus. Sky God.

Tammuz (*Near Eastern*)—Consort of Ishtar. God of the Harvest, agriculture, and love.

Eshu (*African, Yoruba*)—Also knownas LEGBA and BABA (Father), guardian of homes and villages. Trickster, protector, teacher, rules literacy, and divination of the future.

Horus (*Egyptian*)—God of the Living, sacred child of Isis and Osiris. His symbol, THE EYE OF HORUS, represents life within death.

Obatala (*African, Yoruba*)—Father, Creator. He represents clarity, justice, and wisdom, with dominion over hell, peace, and harmony. Also, ruler of everything that is white on Earth (snow, bones, etc.). *Sometimes seen as androgynous—both male and female.*

Drawing the Alignments

Powerful alignments may be effectively drawn with all of our chosen Deities. This is usually accomplished in stages, and it is recommended that at least several weeks be allowed for *each* Alignment to be drawn.

The Alignments are drawn verbally, and repeated as frequently as feels natural—until they ring the Inner Bell. Here is an example:

For Women

Light your Goddess candle, look into the flame, and state this Alignment chant:

I, (*your name*), am Diana Incarnate.
I, (*your name*), am Selene Incarnate.
I, (*your name*), am Hecate Incarnate.

> I, (*your name*), am perfectly aligned with
>   Kernunnos.
>
> I, (*your name*), am perfectly aligned with Pan.

For Men

Light your God candle, look into the flame, and state this Alignment chant:

> I, (*your name*), am Kernunnos Incarnate.
>
> I, (*your name*), am Pan Incarnate.
>
> I, (*your name*), am perfectly aligned with Diana.
>
> I, (*your name*), am perfectly aligned with Selene.
>
> I, (*your name*), am perfectly aligned with Hecate.

If you are a Priestess or Priest of any of the Goddess or God aspects, this will be revealed to you by the time you have finished drawing all of your chosen Alignments. Then you may add:

> I, (*your name*), am Priestess of Diana (*or fill in appropriate title*).

Not everyone chooses this path. For those who do, it is from that point on, usually stated at the beginning of the Alignment chant.

Even after all the Alignments have been clearly drawn, the chant is still repeated when necessary. It is used in most of the work, and also should be repeated whenever a power charge is desired.

Now the basic Words of Power outline, cited previously, is transformed by the Witch into a spell or blessing. This is its full form, with spaces left for you to fill in your appropriate personal Alignments after you have made them yours:

There is One Power
Which is Diana, Selene, Hecate, Kernunnos, and Pan.
And I, (*your name*) am Goddess (God) Incarnate.
l am (*list all Alignments*).
As your Witch (and your Priestess/Priest),
Diana, Selene, Hecate, Kernunnos, and Pan,
I call on You to please help me with this (*fill in*)
to give me (*fill in*)
to bless me (*or name other*) in this (*state specific work*)
Thank you, my Deities.
And so mote it be.

A variation:

There is One Power
Which is Goddess and God,
Which is Diana, Selene, Hecate, Kernunnos, and Pan.
And I, (*your name here*),
Am Diana Incarnate, Selene Incarnate, and Hecate
    Incarnate,
Perfectly aligned with Kernunnos
Perfectly aligned with Pan
I am Witch of Diana, Witch of Selene, Witch of
    Hecate,
Witch of Kernunnos and Witch of Pan.
I am Priestess of (*fill in alignment*)
My Deities hereby work for me and through me
    According to free will and for the good of all
For perfect (*state goal*)
And so mote it be!

If you wish to add a release, it goes right after the goal,
and then the goal is restated:
I hereby release all worry, fear, disbelief, etc. (*name
difficulties*)
And replace this with perfect (*restate goal*)
With thanks.
And so mote it be!

Of course, this process is extremely flexible, and can—
and should—be varied or changed according to what work
is to be done.

Remember, if you specify a form for the goal or manifestation, always add, "its equivalent or better."

Naturally, there are shortened forms. They are equally
effective because *the Alignments have already been drawn.*

You can simply call upon whichever Deity or Deities have
dominion over the particular area for which you are working.
For example:

Diana, You who watch over children, please protect my
child on this journey.
Hecate, You who dispenses all justice, please take care
of my business transactions today.
Selene, You who provide the Infinity of Solution,
please help me manifest a way to solve this apparent
problem.
Kernunnos, You who provide balance, and warmth,
please bless us in our new love relationship.
Pan, You who shape flexibility in all things, please bless
my new writing project.

Or you can call on all Five (or more)—or any combination of Them.

Also, as a sort of daily "Cosmic Vitamin" (or to use as meditation) you may simply say or think to yourself:

Diana, Selene, Hecate, Kernunnos, and Pan, please
   bless me.

Similarly, you can call on any Deity with Whom you are aligned.

As an extension of the statement of your Alignments, you may add this magical affirmation:

I am Priestess (Priest), Witch, and Queen (King) of
   my Realm.

CHAPTER 4

The Tools

Candles

An excellent way to enhance your work is to use candles: A Work candle, a Goddess candle, a God candle, a Water candle, and an Earth candle. (The belief is that the additional elements, Fire and Air, are included in each of all five.) They are placed on the altar, floor, or working table:

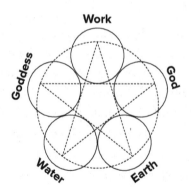

However, one candle at a time may be used for specific purposes, depending on the work.

The Goddess candle is used to draw the Goddess (female) Alignments. The God candle is used to draw the God (male) Alignments.

Basic Consecration of Candles

Even before the Alignments are drawn, each of the candles should be consecrated by the Witch. As you light each candle for the first time, say:

The One Power Which is Goddess and God,
Works for and through me (*your name*), a perfect
 microcosm of the Power.
And l consecrate this candle to the use of Positive
 Magic only,
Positive Witchcraft only,
For the good of all,
And according to free will.
And so mote it be.

Then, after your Alignments are drawn, you may reconsecrate your candles with your Alignment chant (see following section), or you may consecrate new ones as soon as they are purchased, before you use them.

The Work candle is usually plain white and unscented. The Goddess candle is usually white, unscented, or vanilla scented, if desired. The God candle is usually red or orange, often cinnamon scented. Earth and Water candles are colored and scented according to personal Affinities. Follow your Inner Bell.

Note: No candle should ever have been used for any other purpose, and of course all candles should be set aside for the work of Positive Magic only. Feel free to use any additional candles, for any purpose that is meaningful to you. For example: a green candle could be used for the time of planting your garden or to manifest money, and a pink, blue, or yellow candle could be used for conceiving a baby. There are numerous books about Candle Magic. Please use their instructions (and the suggestions here) only according to your inner wisdom, as you choose, with all the variations and innovations you wish.

The Athame

A primary Witchcraft tool is the *athame* or ritual knife. Ideally, it is a knife that has never touched any living being (or any being which once had life, such as meat). If, however, it has been used before—or if you suspect it might have been—then work a blessing to cleanse it.

Cleansing Blessing for an Athame
(*State Alignments, then add*):
With Goddess and God working for and through me,
I hereby release from this, my athame,
All cause, effect, manifestation, form, or essence
Of every and any negative influence, idea, or thought
From all time and all space.
(*to continue, see the Athame Consecration that follows*)

An athame is traditionally sharp threefold: both sides and the point. Some Witches purchase special daggers; some file down and sharpen the duller side of any ordinary kitchen knife or even a letter opener. Actually, filing is usually not necessary, as long as the knife is thin and no side is totally blunt. Of course, it must be kept (or carried) in a sheath or similarly protective enclosure, for purposes of both privacy and safety. It is also best used—or even shown—only in private or in the presence of other Witches.

Consecrate your athame as soon as you get it, and before the first time you use it. An effective technique: Hold it over all five candles, dip its tip in the flame of each, and draw a pentagram with it in the air over the candles, as you say:

Athame Consecration
By Diana, By Selene, By Hecate, By Kernunnos, and
     By Pan,
I (*your name*), Goddess (or God) Incarnate,
(*state all Alignments*),
Hereby consecrate this, my athame, to the Goddess
and the God and to all the work of Positive Witchcraft,
For the Good of All
And according to Free Will.
And so mote it be.

Much specific work is then done by drawing a pentagram in the air over the flame of all five candles using the athame, and stating the appropriate spell or blessing.

Once you have your *physical* athame, you then also have your *invisible* athame, its counterpart. You may hold up the invisible athame (visualize yourself holding it up) whenever you need it, such as in front of you for protection in any potentially threatening situation. Usually at such times, the Witch calls on Hecate—or even all your Deities. Again, use your Inner Bell.

Your physical and/or invisible athame is traditionally used in rituals of banishing, releasing negative influences, and exorcisms. (Well, there's no need to exorcise any devil, because we don't believe in such a being, but on rare occasions, there could be negative influences or pesky entities that should be bade goodbye and good luck.) *Of course, you never touch anything or anyone with it physically.* You hold it up in front of you, draw pentagrams in the air with it—during rituals and other magical workings—and also draw your Circle with it, as well as close the Circle at the finish of your work.

Incense

Incense is used according to the Witch's personal taste. Sometimes, if the candles are strongly scented, incense may not be needed. However, it's a fine aid to concentration, and always reminds us of the element of Air, specifically when used in the Circle indoors. Study a list of herbs, spices, roots, barks, and their traditional meanings, and *when you can, mix your own.* Buy ingredients from any metaphysical supply house, herbal store, or online; even health food stores now carry many helpful herbs. You will also need charcoal, either chips or blocks, to get the flame going. Use a small cauldron, or any suitable container that looks like a cauldron. Cleanse and consecrate everything, of course. An easy and effective alternative is the popular stick incense, which used to be found in head shops and is now available just about anywhere.

Pendulum

A pendulum can provide a quick and portable oracle for the Witch. However, it only answers questions with a yes or a no, and it only answers *for the present*, so remember that the answer is subject to change over time, or with a shift of perception.

A pendulum should be small and relatively lightweight. A crystal bead is ideal. It should be just heavy enough to swing freely from its cord. The pendulum cord can be made of thin string, embroidery silk, fishing line, or even a slender jewelry chain, as long as it is light enough to swing freely, strong enough not to break easily, and flexible enough not to kink or readily form knots. The cord should be approximately 10 inches long. If you prefer it longer or shorter, you will know after a few rounds of questions. Some New Age and occult shops sell ready-made pendulums, which are fine, especially if they have not been used before.

Always cleanse and consecrate your pendulum when you get it (or make it) before its first use. Some Witches like to breathe on it as part of the consecration. This is a personal touch. Keep your pendulum on your altar, preferably wrapped in some favorite little cloth or pouch. You may want to carry it around with you in your pocket or purse. Try to keep it wrapped to screen out distracting vibrations, and do not let anyone else use it. Others may ask it questions, but you are always the one who holds it.

To use your pendulum, hold the cord lightly between thumb and forefinger. Ask your question in a form that is suitably answered with a yes or a no. The query may be aloud or silent. Do not move your hand. The pendulum will move by itself (that is the whole idea). I have found that, for me, it will swing back and forth for a yes answer and in a circular motion for a no. This is the most popular movement. However, your pendulum may move differently. Experiment for a while to determine how it works for you. A helpful technique is to ask the pendulum, "What is your movement for a *yes?*" Next, ask it, "What is your movement for a *no?*" This should be repeated several times until you are sure of your pendulum's response. The movements will appear to be combined if the matter is not yet decided, or if the answer is literally yes and no (let's face it, some answers are).

Remember that an answer given by a pendulum, as with any other personal oracle, is subject to change with time, and can also be changed by careful Words of Power work. As always, the future can be changed, problems averted before they occur, dangers avoided, and any situation transformed and turned to good. Work your Words of Power with the goal of positive transformation—and ask again.

How does a pendulum work? Some say there is a special spirit of the pendulum, which expresses itself through the swing. Another theory is that the user plugs into the Collective Unconscious, where all knowledge and answers reside. Another theory: We each tap our own personal inner wisdom when we concentrate on the pendulum's swing. Or— the pendulum is an expression of our own powers of *telekinesis,* the art of making inanimate objects move. Or do our own resident spirits help out? Ask your pendulum!

Crystals

Today, not only Witches, but many other people work with crystals, and numerous books on the subject are surfacing as the Aquarian Age evolves. Certain crystals are believed to have certain properties, certain affinities with certain people, colors, musical notes, astrological signs, and other specific meanings.

As with the specific, traditional meanings often ascribed to tarot cards—all-purpose meanings, which I believe are so limiting—I consider any rigid definitions of the properties of crystals to be inappropriate for a Witch. Like animals and people, crystals are unique, living beings. Each one is a special entity, unlike any other. There is simply no way to label or define their properties.

Crystals are alive. Their individual life span is longer than ours, in linear time, and their vital functions are so much slower than ours—so that to the uninitiated, crystals may seem not to be alive at all. But all you need to do is meditate on a crystal, hold it in your hand, or talk to it, and you will see that it is indeed a living being. Thus the Witch deals with crystals as living beings—not as tools, but as friends.

You may accumulate many crystals in your lifetime. You may keep them on your altar, or in important places around your home. Smaller ones may be carried with you, or even incorporated into jewelry. When you feel you need a crystal, most likely, one will appear in your life. Nowadays we buy our crystals in shops or online and we exchange them as gifts. It is truly a remarkable gift of the Earth to find a crystal in nature.

Because a crystal is so old and has probably had many influences before it reached you, I recommend that you cleanse it as soon as you get it. You may rinse it in clear water and then hold it over your candles, as you consecrate it with Words of Power before it lives with you. Consecrate it according to free will and for the good of all, and dedicate it to Positive Witchcraft and Positive Magic only.

Cleansing and Consecration for a Crystal
With Goddess and God
Working for and through me
And for and through this crystal,
According to Free Will and For The Good of All
I give thanks for this crystal entity
And help to cleanse it of every and any negative influ-
ence, idea, vibration, thought,
experience, or problem that might have touched it in all
time and all space.
And I now consecrate this crystal
To the work of Positive Magic and Positive Witchcraft
only.
And so mote it be.

Spend time with each crystal and allow it to reveal to you what its purpose is in your life. You may find that it actually speaks to you. The messages may be as clear as those of a spirit voice, or the message may be subtler. Often, a specific crystal is meant to work with you in a specific way. For example, one crystal may sit vigil as protection, another may help guard against disease, another may aid in healing, another may help with psychic work, spells, or divination. Crystals can actually converse with you, reveal mental images, give advice or comfort; their functions are as diverse as those of myriad friends.

Be open, work Words of Power for revelations of each crystal's appropriate purpose in your life, and please do not allow any preconceptions to interfere with the magic of crystals for you.

At times, a crystal may indicate to you that it needs to go to someone else. Do not hesitate to give that crystal to the right person. If you find that you want a crystal for a specific purpose in your life, work Words of Power to call the right crystal to you. And if you feel that any crystal does not really belong with you, follow its direction as well as your own inner voice as to the best way to release that crystal out of your life.

When my coven meets, we spread out quite a beautiful array of everyone's crystals in the work area alongside the candles. We feel the crystals' power join with ours in the work. Recently, we have purchased some beautiful crystal and silver wands to use as actual athames, a variation on traditional knives.

Crystals echo and reveal the multitude of forms found in nature. So, looking into a crystal can truly give you an amazing amount of information about the rest of our world. And don't forget the famous crystal ball! *Scrying*—looking into a clear object to see the future or view other dimensions—is a favorite activity for both crystal and Witch. The good news is that scrying need not be limited to crystal balls. Numerous other crystal shapes can help out.

At various times, crystals like sunlight, moonlight, candlelight, and water. All other information for their care and power I leave for your crystals to tell you.

Other Witch's tools include tarot cards, runestones, and oracles from various cultures, such as *cowrie shells* and *The I Ching*. For scrying, traditional tools are crystal balls, so-called Witches' Balls, and the Witch's Mirror (an all black mirror). An old-fashioned method of scrying is to peer into a glass or black bowl of water and oil. Cleanse and consecrate, as previously directed.

As for herbs, suffice it to say that it's best to grow and gather them yourself. When you use them, check the phases of the Moon. Herbs are adjuncts, only.

Jewelry

Silver is the metal of the Goddess and the Moon.
Gold is the metal of the Horned God and the Sun.

Please try to buy your jewelry from a place that does not sell anything that is meant to be used for Negative Magic. Satanic magic is obvious, but some Ceremonial work—or even some alleged Witchcraft work—may be manipulative. If you have any doubt about your jewelry's origins, especially if it was ever worn or used before, do a cleansing blessing on it to release all negative influences and then consecrate it to your Deities.

A silver encircled pentagram on a silver chain is best worn at all times. High Priestesses and High Priests may wear an extra pentagram—also silver and encircled—larger than the everyday one, for ritual purposes. Some pentagrams have crystals or jewels in their design.

It is advisable for women to have a Goddess ring—silver, showing the face of the Goddess—to be worn on the pointing finger (first finger) of the right hand if right-handed, left hand if left-handed. Draw pentagrams in the air with this finger, and touch beings for purposes of blessing with this ring, usually when the physical athame is not with you, or when you want a "gentler" blessing or Circle drawing. Some men may also wear a Goddess ring. This is a personal matter.

Art Nouveau—styled depictions of the Goddess are popular and easy to find in rings, even in non-Craft jewelry stores. Also available are other well known Goddess images: The Venus of Willendorf, the Creten Snake Goddess, the Moon Goddess, and others. Trust your Inner Bell for your choice.

Both men and women wear Horned God rings or bracelets: silver circles with two touching rams' or goats' heads. Some rings of the Horned One are made of ivory or horn. In such a case, please bless the animal it came from, and release it of negative influences (both the jewelry and the animal, according to its Free Will).

Consecrate all your jewelry as you did your athame, holding it over the flame of one or all of your five candles. Goddess jewelry often gets held for an extra "dose" over the Goddess candle, and God jewelry over the God candle.

Once consecrated, anything or anyone you touch with your pentagram or your rings becomes imbued and blessed with that Power.

Any additional jewelry with Witchcraft motifs, such as silver crescent Moons or gold Suns, and Goddess or God pendants may be worn according to personal taste and budget, but are not necessary. Cleanse and consecrate everything when you get it, before the first wearing. Expensive ritual regalia such as crowns and jewels are enjoyed by some, but not necessary for the work.

Your Witch jewelry is your guide, your protection, and your reminder of the Deities and Their work. As with all Craft symbols, the jewelry also has its invisible counterparts, which are always with you.

CHAPTER 5

The Coven

A coven consists of thirteen or fewer members whose harmonies work well together. My preference is that the group be guided solely by perfect love and perfect trust. I believe this is so powerful that no rules, obligations, by-laws, or guidelines, other than this, are necessary.

I also believe that there are no proscribed ways for a coven of this tradition to be formed, except by mutual consent. New members may be brought in if everyone agrees to this. Although many Witches may prefer formal initiation, I believe that none is necessary. However, the new member should be provided with reading material and ample explanations of the work. Not every coven contains a High Priestess and/or High Priest, but if either one exists in a group, some may hold elections, take turns, or spontaneously agree on the choices. Children of members may participate according to their free will only, with no coercion. (*"Oh Mom, do I have to do magic again, tonight?"*)

If you do not have a coven, and you wish to become part of one, you may send out a *Coven Call* to draw the right coven to you, or to manifest the perfect one. Use your Inner Bell to determine whether you want to form a new coven or to become part of an already existing one. Do not specify exactly which coven—if such already exists—as that would be manipulative, of course. Just describe the type of coven you want, adding "its equivalent or better." State your Alignment chants first, and then send out the Call for "the most perfect coven members and other Witches to work with in a perfect exchange of Perfect Love and Perfect Mutual Trust, understanding, and Positive work." Do this during the New Moon, the Waxing Moon, the Full Moon—or all three. As in most work, you may use all five candles and your athame.

When a new coven is formed, it should be blessed by all the members. Existing covens may renew the blessing at each meeting.

Coven Blessing
With Goddess and God working for and through
    us all,
As I am Priestess of (*name Deity*),
(*each Witch states primary alignment*)
We are all our Goddesses Incarnate,
We are all perfectly Aligned with our Gods,
We are all Gods/Incarnate,
We are all perfectly Aligned with our Goddesses,
We are Witches of all our Goddesses and Gods.
We hereby bless our coven
And dedicate ourselves as a group and individually

To the work of Positive Magic and Positive Witchcraft
   only
According to Free Will
And for the Good of All
And so mote it be.

The coven meets on the holidays (the Eight Sabbats), to celebrate and to work, and any other time that all the members choose to meet. Meetings may take place at the home of a member, at the homes of all or several members, or at outdoor sites agreeable to all—or any other place that is private, feels right, and is convenient for all members. Coven members who cannot attend are mentioned, along with their requests, as part of the work and a place in the Circle may be set aside for them. There is no required attendance. The group as a whole decides when and where it will meet. It is, in my opinion, best to meet at night *on* each holiday, not during that week. But again, this is up to the coven's discretion, taking into consideration other obligations, and how many members are able to attend. Time and space become flexible with this work. There is no judgment on those who cannot attend—all you have to do is set the approximate time for the work to begin and invite the absent members to "plug in" mentally. Some groups work over the Internet or by phone.

If, over a linear time period, any members drift away from the group, this is a natural process and usually has mutual consent, with no blame or guilt. If, however, any personal problems between any members arise, the matter should be blessed by the entire group for peaceful and loving resolution, to Turn It To Good (unless the involved members wish to handle it by themselves). Personal philosophy, styles of work, or individual harmonies may sometimes cause a coven to split into two separate ones. Ideally, there is no rivalry between members or covens, and there is certainly no slander or gossip.

The coven as a whole decides what to do about the attendance of outsiders. Secrecy was once essential to Witchcraft for obvious reasons of safety, but times have changed immeasurably for the better. For this we give thanks. However, as a general guiding principle, it is still best not to have non-Witches present at the Sabbats. In some covens, an exception is made in the case of spouses or close loved ones. In general, it is a better idea instead to hold *Esbats* at specific times—such as on the Full, or New Moon—and use these times to include such outsiders. There are always exceptions, but when outsiders are present, their lack of belief and/or understanding could interfere with the work. It cannot stop or negate the work, but it could slow it down in linear time, or act as an inhibiting influence.

It is generally the responsibility of the High Priestess or High Priest to arrange each meeting, to call the members, and either bring the tools or to designate someone to do so.

Coven Meetings

Each coven meeting is a joyous celebration. If possible, there is a celebratory meal, with food either contributed by all or provided by the various members in a fair and rotating fashion. Wine and cakes are the ritual refreshments. My coven has always preferred to order in Chinese food—our favorite. For all the pleasantries and fun, when it's time to work, things can get pretty serious.

We work in darkness, lit only by consecrated flame.
All the work is done in Circle.

The members sit or stand in a Circle, facing inward. The traditional size of the Circle is nine feet in diameter, because nine is the essential multiple of three, symbolizing that all the work is done Threefold. However, this too is flexible according to your space, coven size, and comfort. At outdoor meetings, it is often more comfortable to work standing, and stones may be set up beforehand to mark the Circle. The candles (or, if outdoors, possibly the bonfire) are in the Circle's center. If incense is used, it too is in the center, along with plants, seasonal foliage, crystals, and any other tools. You may use all five candles, or more, or just the Work candle.

The High Priest lights the flame (if there is a High Priest. (Otherwise, another appropriate member does so.)

The High Priestess consecrates the Circle with her athame, including all the members in her gesture and forming a pentagram in the air between them. Some covens draw an invisible Circle on the ground with a stick or wand. So powerful is this circumference, that a Witch who wishes to exit the Circle— even temporarily—will draw an "opening" on the ground to walk through. Then, on re-entry, the Circle is connected again.

Because it is essential to understand fully all words, spells, and chants, it is recommended that they be composed on the spot for all work. The Alignment chant is made, and the following, or some variation on it, may be spoken by the High Priestess:

Opening Circle Consecration
By Diana, By Selene, By Hecate,
By Kernunnos, and By Pan,
I hereby consecrate this Circle
And everyone in it
For the work of this (*name Sabbat*)
Which represents (*fill in meaning of Sabbat*),
For the Good of All
And according to Free Will.
The Power that moves the Moon Moves all of us.
The Power that lights the Sun Lights all our lives.
Even if we do not state all the work
We wish to do this Holiday,
All the work is done.

Usually, no one says "and so mote it be" yet because the work then continues. But some choose to say "so mote it be" after each segment of the work.

In my coven, we work for each member Witch first, passing the Work candle (and/or an athame) clockwise. We feel this immediately strengthens each of us for further work. Sometimes we discuss the work to be done that evening. Next, we perform healings and honor other requests by outsiders, if we agree to this. We conclude with a blessing for our city, country, planet—and beyond—stating specific goals: Peace, an end to suffering, environmental safety, help for troubled areas, etc. Often we raise a Cone of Power.

Every coven works out its own agenda and best procedures. Just remember that whenever working for outsiders, you must do so according to Free Will and for the Good of All only, and only at their direct personal request. Helping the community is a Witchcraft tradition. However, we do not advertise our work nor seek people to help. And we never expect payment. Those who are ready for our help seek us, and their privacy is assured.

Passing the Candle

One excellent technique is to sit in Circle and pass the Work candle clockwise from each coven member to the next. The candle is placed in front of each Witch for as long as she/he needs it; that is, the Witch states all the manifestations she/he gives thanks for, and names all the personal goals to be worked for. The Witch may also hold an athame; sometimes we pass that around instead of the candle. Included also is blessing work for immediate loved ones and familiars. As we focus on each Witch, other members join in, silently, with their energies, willing the work to manifest and asking the Goddess and the God to make it happen. If the Witch who is being thus focused on wants to work entirely in silence, or to become silent at any point, the others continue to focus and to bless silently that whatever is being worked for will manifest, even if they do not consciously know what it is. If the Witch who is being focused on invites help, any other member of the coven may speak up and suggest additional goals to manifest. When each Witch feels completion in his/her work, the candle or athame is then passed to the next Witch. This is also a time to include absent members, and the candle or athame may then be passed and held in the place where they usually sit.

The Four Directions

Some Witches open their Circles by calling on the Four Directions, also known as the Four Corners. A version of this work may also be found in Native American ritual. My coven has somehow just not gotten into this practice on a regular basis, but if it feels right to you, you might want to look in other Witchcraft books or work it out for yourself, in your own way. The important thing is to acknowledge North, East, South, and West, and turn to face each one. Covens in which I have been a guest have started with something like this: Turning to the North, "*Spirits of the North, welcome. We call on you to Bless our Circle.*" Turning to the East, "*Spirits of the East, welcome. Please join and bless our Circle.*" And so forth. The two important things to remember are to always proceed in a clockwise direction and to thank the Four Direction spirits at the end. When you close the Circle, again, "*Spirits of the North, hail and farewell. Spirits of the East, hail and farewell . . . etc. Thank you and Be Blessed.*" Something similar to that. This is an effective way to establish your Circle in Time and Space. Some groups also acknowledge Nature Spirits or Spirits of the Elements. I often work with the Elements myself. It goes something like this: "*Spirits of Fire, bless our Circle.*" Then call in Air, Earth, and Water in the same manner. And at the end, "*Hail and farewell . . .*" to each.

Visualizing in the Coven

This is an amplification of the previous work. When the candle or athame is passed, the Witch who is being focused on states something such as:

> I ask you all now to please visualize for me the goal I am working for. Picture my new home, even though it seems as though I have not yet found it in The World of Form. Picture me in it, help me to see it . . .

And the others all close their eyes and allow images to come into their consciousnesses at each request. When a Witch "sees" any positive version of the requested image, she/he states it aloud, in as much detail as possible. For example:

> I see you, (name), in your new home. I see you standing and looking out your window, which is tall and arched. There is a view of trees, with a gentle breeze blowing the curtain . . . you're smiling, and you're saying, "This feels right."

Others may join in and expand upon each image. The goal is to have the entire coven simultaneously visualizing the desired manifestation. If the Witch who is being focused on wants any changes, she/he states them. If anything negative, any limitation, block, or Form Contingency comes into view—it is stated, acknowledged, stripped of all negative power, released, and replaced with a positive Affinity and image.

For healing, if a Witch is afflicted, that witch may move to the center of the Circle, and the candle or athame may be passed to the Witch. In healing, the visualization may become more symbolic. For example:

> I picture tiny little women running through (*name*)'s
> bones, carrying soft and gentle brushes. When they
> come to the seemingly broken area, they rub their little
> brushes softly over it until the edges knit together
> so perfectly that you cannot see where a break ever
> existed.

The use of magical helpers is effective in healing visualization, but no matter what the image is, remember to always use *gentle* images for healing—for flow of blood and energy, healing of tissue and bone, for muscle and organ repair, and for dissolution of anything which has been labeled as harmful. *Always* preface any diagnostic label with a disclaimer, "seemingly" or "that which has been called" to strip it of any and all negative power. For example:

> I picture silver rain water washing away that which has
> been called a growth in (*name*)'s chest, until his (her)
> entire body is sparkling, clean, and free of any bumps,
> no matter how small . . .

Always end on a positive statement and image of total wholeness and health.

Visualization may also be used for any outsider or friend for whom the Circle works.

The Cone of Power

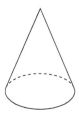

This is not always used, and it is used only for specific, requested purposes upon which the whole coven agrees. It is usually the final work of the night. The High Priestess (if there is one) leads this work, stating the Alignment chants of all, as well as for herself, and calling upon the Deities to guide and help the coven.

The High Priest may join in, as well as other members. It is helpful to name the exact address of the destination, or at least the general geographical location where the Cone is to touch down. The purpose is stated as specifically as possible. However, we can also raise a "general" cone.

All the Witches focus on the visual image of the Cone rising and flying to its destination. Sometimes this can be seen physically. Often, the Cone rises almost automatically as the work is begun, but it may be necessary to raise the Power (actually to activate the energy and the Power) first. There are several ways to do this:

1. Coven members sit or stand holding hands and "pass the Power" clockwise through each Witch's body, out the hand and arm, and into the hand, arm, and body of the Witch on the left. The signal for the energy passing is a squeeze of the hand. The energy starts at a naturally slow pace and accelerates more and more until it is moving through the Circle so quickly that it must be let out. Everyone will recognize this point in linear time. The High Priestess calls out her directive to send it out, now—and all visualize the

Cone rising and sailing forth to its destination. We raise our arms over our heads for this, and feel the energy rush out through our hands and fingers. We conclude, "And so mote it be!"

2. Coven members dance hand— in—hand, clockwise. Some covens dance without holding hands, but I feel it's best to contain the energy by physical contact before it's sent out. The dance accelerates until the energy can no longer be contained in the Circle, and the High Priestess calls out the directive, and all stop dancing to visualize the Cone moving up and out. As above, arms are raised, fingers extended— "And so mote it be!"

3. With all the members standing still, the Power may be drawn up out of the ground, through the feet of each Witch and out through the top of the shoulders and heads. It is, again, best to join hands for this, and all hands know when to let go as the High Priestess or another Witch calls out the release—and the Cone sails up and outward, and so mote it be.

Of course, you may use any other method that works for your group to raise the Power: Dancing, chanting, drumming, or even shaking party noisemakers. After the Cone is raised, it is usually best to sit or lie down in the Circle and relax.

Closing the Circle

The High Priestess, or another Witch, closes the Circle by drawing it clockwise with her athame and drawing pentagrams over the flame and in the center between the Witches. Here is a typical closing—subject to your changes.

High Priestess: By Diana, By Selene, By Hecate, By
Kernunnos, and By Pan.
I hereby close this Circle,
And give thanks for the work that is done.
All: And so mote it be!

The High Priest (or another Witch) blows out the flame or all join in.

Cakes and wine or other desserts are enjoyed, and coven matters are discussed. Do not dilute the work with statements of doubt or worry. Celebrate, dance, sing, and/or tell jokes. As in ancient times:

Merry meet,
Merry part.

CHAPTER 6

The Holidays

Always mark the holidays, even if you must do so solitary. It is a joy when the coven can meet on the holidays, but the work may be done no matter where you are or who is able to join you. Sometimes the coven must meet "around" or "approximately" at the time of a holiday; if so, try to work solitary or with another Witch (or even with another Witch over the phone) or with another Witch or Witches in spirit—or with a spirit or spirits, right on the holiday. Try to take even a moment, no matter how busy you are. Of course, this must not inconvenience you nor can it interfere with the rest of your life. Do not force, but allow time and space to become flexible for you. Any feelings of obligation about celebrating and meeting on the holidays is a contemporary pitfall to which the religion of Witchcraft need not succumb. Unless it feels natural, spontaneous, organic, and right to celebrate, to meet, and to work on a holiday, the very meaning of it can be lost and you might as well forget the whole thing. Remember, Witchcraft is emphatically not an organized religion.

Whenever you mark a holiday, you are working with, and tuning in to (if you want to) an infinite number of other Witches, Pagans, Priestesses, Priests, Magicians, and Wizards, in all time and all space, from many lifetimes past and present. You may be solitary, but you are never alone.

The reason to work at these times is that, on Earth, the magic and the Power are most intense for specific purposes because of energy flows, planet rotation, gravitational pulls and balances, and astrological configurations, as well as the previously mentioned cumulative participation. These times are also celebrated by most other Pagans in the West. For the Witch, the meanings of these times are even more specific than the more popular traditional theme of each holiday.

For the Equinoxes and the Solstices, try to work exactly on the astrological moment of the changeover from one astrological sign to the next. If this is not possible, then work as close to the moment *before* it occurs in linear time. The night before is always fine.

Night or day? We may *celebrate* during the day—and this is often traditional, such as on Beltane (Mayday)—but for the magical work itself, we meet in darkness and at night.

Whether Witches choose to work robed, dressed, undressed (skyclad), or in costume is *a form*. Whatever the choice, remember Free Will. Everything in the work is voluntary—or it does not work.

Specific Meanings of the Holidays

The traditional meanings of the Eight Sabbats may be found in many places: Doreen Valiente's work, my own *Positive Magic*, *The Ancient/Modern Witch*, astrological calendars, books, and websites galore. The specific holiday meanings for the Witch are:

Dec. 20–23: *The Midwinter Solstice (Yule)*: Rebirth as the Wheel turns anew. Overcome depression and despair.

Feb. 2: *Candlemas: Cthonic emergence*—the first stirrings of life in darkness beneath the Earth. Harbinger of Spring and good for "seedlings" of all sorts, including projects, this is the Cross-Quarter Day between the Winter Solstice and the Spring Equinox. (Also known as Lughnesad, Bridget's Day, and Groundhog Day!)

March 20–23: *Spring or Vernal Equinox:* Equal day and equal night, equal female and equal male, equal Darkness and Light. Good for Sex Magic, and for balancing. Eggs will literally stand on end.

May 1: *Beltane:* Celebrate the flowering and fertility of The Goddess. Good for conception and Birth Magic. Leap on your brooms over tilled fields—or any plant. This is the Cross-Quarter Day between the Spring Equinox and the Midsummer Solstice.

June 20–23: *Midsummer Solstice:* The Horned God is at the peak of His manifest Power, and the flowering Goddess welcomes Him. Good for Sex Magic: The female takes in and is nourished by the male—and the male is reenergized thereby.

Aug. 2: *Lammas:* The First Harvest. Give thanks and name goals for the next two harvests. This is the Cross-Quarter Day between the Midsummer Solstice and the Fall Equinox.

Sept. 20–23: *Fall or Autumnal Equinox:* Equal night and equal day, equal male and equal female, equal Darkness and equal Light. Good for Sex Magic, good for balancing. The Second Harvest—give thanks and name goals to build toward the next harvest.

Oct. 31: *Halloween (Samhain)*: Celebrate the triumph of eternal life over physical death. The veil between the Two Worlds is thin, and loved ones from the Invisible World join in the work and celebration. A good time to work for future reincarnation with loved ones, always according to Free Will and for the Good of All. This is the Third and final Harvest of The Wheel of The Year, and the Cross-Quarter Day between the Fall Equinox and the Midwinter Solstice. Give thanks, and know that the harvests repeat threefold through all the years.

Seasonal foliage, fruits, vegetables, etc. may be used in the Circle for each Sabbat, but never harm a living plant!

CHAPTER 7

Moon Work

The New Moon and the Waxing Moon

The time of the New Moon and the Waxing Moon is traditionally ruled by Diana. The New Moon lasts only a moment, but Her influence extends through the entire Waxing period, which is the following two weeks up until the Full Moon. The New Moon marks new beginnings, and this meaning extends through the next two weeks as a time of nourishment, growth, and rebirth. Projects, thoughts, contacts, ideas, and new ventures may be started and directed *outward*. Magic may be worked for drawing, attracting, manifesting, and beginning.

Some Witches work on the moment of the New Moon or slightly thereafter, but She is not visible to the physical eye at these times. However, if you really tune in, you can actually feel the moment that the Dark Moon gives way to the New Moon. The exact astrological moment is found in almanacs and in any good astrological calendar or ephemeris. You may use the

Goddess candle for such work, and though you may work as usual with all the Deities, at this time, call specifically to Diana—or your chosen representative of the New Moon.

The Full Moon

The time of the Full Moon is the time of Selene. Although the actual moment of the Full Moon lasts for just that—a moment—the Full Moon time is a seven-day period extending three days before the Full Moon day and three days after it.

> Before the change, three days
> After the change, three days
> Good Fortune.
>
> —*The I Ching*, Hexagram 57
> Nine in the 5th place

The quality to work with at this time is the Infinity of Solution. The actual work is Drawing Down the Moon, which may be done solitary, with another Witch, or in a group. You may join with another or others mentally, but it is best to set this up beforehand. You may even work with another Witch over the phone. Again, you are never alone, because at this time, just as on the Sabbats, Witches of all time and space join in the work, linking Moon Power to Earth.

If possible, look at the Moon during this linear time period, and try to watch Her expression, which can provide for you a quality of focus for the coming month. Try to listen for Her message to you.

It is best, if possible, to Draw Down the Moon at *exactly* the moment of Her fullest. The precise time may be found in calendars, almanacs, astrological transits, online, and sometimes even in a local newspaper's weather section or under the information on the tides. If the timing of your Full Moon work is not possible because of schedules—including sleep—then draw Her down *as close* to the moment as possible, before the Full Moon. Before going to sleep, simply instruct your subconscious mind to do the work at the right moment. When in doubt, draw Her down on the night of (and before) the Full Moon. If you are out in the World of Form at the moment of the Full Moon, take a moment to pause and connect with Her mentally, and be aware of the time.

If possible, draw Her down outdoors (in privacy, of course), in full view of Her face. If you are indoors, try to see Her through a window, and use your Goddess candle to embody Her light. Outdoors, you may also use a candle, if it's not too windy, or place one in a tall container. Stand as directly under Her as you can. If the night is cloudy, try to approximate where She is, and face Her location in the sky.

Draw Her Power into you with your athame. Specifically, draw a pentagram over Her face (or over the candle flame), then reach your athame up to where the Moon resides—no matter where you are, indoors or out—and draw your athame down in a straight line to the area of your heart, lightly touching your chest with its tip.

Suggested Moon Magic
State Alignments—then add:
By the One Power
Acting for me and through me (us)
   I hereby Draw Down The Moon—

And the Power that moves the Moon—
Into myself (into us all)
According to Free Will and for the Good of All
Diana, Selene, Hecate, *enter me (us) now!*
I hereby Draw Down The Moon for:
(*list any specific work, its equivalent or better*)
Thank you, Diana,
Thank you, Selene,
Thank you, Hecate.
The Power that moves the Moon moves through
    me (us) always—
Through all time and all space.
And so mote it be!

Full Moon Lists

Every third Full Moon, we like to write a list of all that we have in our lives, for which to give thanks, and write a list of all in life that we wish to attain. Note that your goals include forms-in-essence: forms including *their equivalents or better.* Keep your lists in your own Book of Shadows, or journal, or some other appropriate place.

By comparing your lists over the Moons as they pass in linear time, it is important to acknowledge each manifestation as it comes to pass, to give thanks for it, and to *enjoy it.*

The Goddess wants us to be happy. It is upon the happiness we experience with each gift that She builds the foundation for future gifts.

On each List Moon, you may refer to your list in detail when you Draw Down The Moon. Or you may simply mention it ("my list"), and its fulfillment as your goal for that time period. All that is on your list may not manifest specifically during each three-month segment in linear time, but over the years of your life, you will note the progression of wishes that come true.

List Moons

My first List Moon was January 1986, and I calculated every third Full Moon from there. However, please feel free to choose your first List Moon *whenever you wish*, whenever you feel it's appropriate, and calculate every third Full Moon from that time. It really doesn't matter when you start. Just remember that approximately every three years, a month contains two Full Moons, the second popularly known as a "Blue Moon." So take this into account in your listings.

And if you wish to designate *every Full Moon* a List Moon, that is fine, too. Or work out your own sequences. The lists are mainly to keep us focused on our Moon Magic.

The Waning Moon and the Dark of The Moon

The Waning Moon is the time of Hecate, and the Dark of The Moon is the time of Hecate's greatest Power. The Waning is the two-week period following the Full, and the Dark lasts just for a moment, although the sky appears to be dark for several nights toward the end of the waning period. The work to be done on both the Waning and the Dark is the work of Hecate's domain, which includes introspection, planning, going back over details and selecting and discarding; dealing with physical death, banishing, releasing, setting up protective shields, and working backward in time. Although you may work with several Deities, call specifically upon Hecate (or an equivalent choice of Deity) for this work.

For working backward in time, use the concept that your perception in the present can change that which seems to have already happened in linear time. This is an excellent opportunity to allow "new facts of history" to reveal themselves. A great example: Native American Indians now prove, through their enlightened present perception, that they were not villains in the past, and the popular view of history shifts forever.

The time of the Dark is excellent for closure, for bringing things to full Circle before New Beginnings.

CHAPTER 8

Cord and String Magic

The idea behind Cord Magic is to embrace and preserve specific attributes of Moon Power, which are available during a specific phase of the Moon. These attributes are directed into a length of cord and held there by knots; thus the attributes are available to the Witch at any time. For example, you may want to perform some magic that is appropriate for the Waxing Moon, such as beginning a new project. Ideally, you would be wisest to wait until after the Moon is New to utilize the most compatible energies for your work. But what if you have good reasons not to wait, and what if—in linear time—up in the sky, the Moon is actually waning? No problem, if you have prepared a New Moon cord! By placing the cord on your altar as you work, you can actually draw upon the New Moon Power at any time of any month.

You can prepare a cord during each phase of the Moon, and thus have available to you the Power of each phase. However, I strongly suggest that you use the cords only when absolutely necessary, and try to work with the phases of the Moon in the sky whenever you can.

To prepare a Moon Cord, use a length of colored yarn about two feet long. You can have five different colors if you prefer, and prepare five different cords: New, Waxing, Full, Waning, and Dark. Or you can simplify matters and use three colors for three cords: New and Waxing combined, Full (alone), Waning and Dark combined. At the time of this writing, I find it sufficient to work with three.

To prepare a cord during the appropriate Moon phase, you may light your Goddess candle and sit at your altar or worktable—or go outside and work under the Moon. Do this work in private or with other Witches. State your Alignments, and call on that Aspect of the Goddess who rules the phase you wish to put into the cord. This is called charging the cord. Thus, for the New and Waxing, call upon Diana; for the Full, call upon Selene; and for the Waning and Dark, call upon Hecate—or of course, you may use any Goddess names that have corresponding meanings for you. It's a good idea to use your athame for this, as the process is related to Drawing Down the Moon. In a sense, you are drawing Her down for each phase to enter your cord, so you may draw a pentagram over the face of the Moon, or over the candle flame that represents Her, and then trace a line of Power from the Moon or flame into your cord, stating Words of Power for your charge.

Suggested Cord for the New and Waxing Moon
(Fill in appropriate Goddess Name for each Moon phase)
(*State Alignments, then add:*)

By the One Power
Working for and through me
   I hereby call on You, Diana,
To enter this cord with Your Power
   To charge this cord
Enter this cord
Stay in this cord
For the Good of All
And according to Free Will
For the work of Positive Witchcraft only
To aid me in my work
At the appropriate times,
According to Your will
As these knots are tied . . .

Then *tie nine knots in the cord*, placing them equidistant from one another and using the ninth knot to tie the cord into a circle, and conclude:

So Mote It Be!

Place this circle on the altar encircling your Goddess candle and leave it there for a while, meditating, if you wish, on the phase of the Moon with which you have charged the cord. When you feel your work is complete, wind the cord into a compact little entity and enclose it in a tiny pouch or box. This is kept on the altar. You may take it with you to coven meetings, or when visiting and working with another Witch, but it's best kept near your candles and tools.

When you work with a Moon Cord, either hold it in your hand or encircle it around your Goddess candle, as you do the specific magic for which you need its aid. When you are finished, put it back in its holder. You may take it out and hold it under the Moon during its name phase, to recharge it, but this is not absolutely essential. There is no drain on Moon Power, such as with a battery. The Power is in the Moon Cord to stay.

Holiday Cords

In addition to Moon Cords, sometimes my coven and I prepare Cords during a special holiday ritual, such as Halloween, tied in appropriately colored yarn. We do this work in our Circle, holding the cords over our candles and blessing them. This perpetuates the meaning and the Power of the holiday into our daily lives. We all enjoy wearing the Cords on our wrists for a few days after the holiday, and then keep them on our personal altars for as long as we like.

String Magic

String Magic is used to retrieve lost objects, but can also be used for missing persons or animals, according to Free Will, of course.

String Magic is performed at the altar, or at a comfortable table or desk. You will need a piece of string to cover the width of your working surface (actually just a little longer), your Work candle (or candle of your choice), and a small piece of paper. We have found the handiest string to be thin white cord such as one used at bakeries or for kites, but any string will do if it's not too thick or stiff. Knitting or needlepoint yarn is fine, as is thin ribbon. You must be able to wind your string tightly at the final step.

Sit at your table and write the name of the lost object on the piece of paper, adding "its equivalent or better." Sometimes we seem to "lose" something because the time has come for it to be replaced by something even more wonderful. If the object of retrieval is a living being, add "According to Free Will and for the Good of All." Carefully fold the paper into a shape approximately 4 inches long and 1½ inches wide.

This piece of paper now represents the object (or being) you wish to call back to you.

Light your candle and place it in the center of the table. Tie one end of the string around the paper, and hold the other end of the string in your hand. Carefully toss the paper end of the string to the end of the table opposite from where you are sitting. You may use either the length or the width of the table, as you prefer, as long as the paper is opposite you, and the candle is in between.

Now, pull the paper end of the string toward you, slowly, with the utmost concentration on that piece of paper *as the object*. Say Words of Power to this effect or any appropriate variation (you may choose to say the longer form, saying all of your Alignments):[1]

By Diana, Selene, Hecate, Kernunnos, and Pan,
whose Priest(ess) and Witch I am, I hereby call back
to me my (state object) which is mine by right of my
consciousness . . .

Concentrate, using One-Point Concentration. That paper becomes the object and it is returning to you now. Close your eyes if this helps. Visualize the paper as the object. As you pull the string in, continue chanting:

> This (*state object*), which is mine, returns to me now,
> through all time and all space, with ease and with joy,
> according to Free Will and for the Good of All . . .

The imagery of this work is much like fishing. You cast the string out; you reel it back. As you pull it in, you may prefer to wind the string around your finger or around your hand.

Concentrate on the object's return until the paper has come into your hand. Then hold it for a moment, eyes closed, picturing—feeling—the object itself in your hand. Do not end your Words of Power until you actually perceive the reality of this. Then end it:

> This (*state object*) is hereby back with me now.
> Thank you, Goddess and God.
> And so mote it be.

Next, wind the string around the piece of paper, making a compact little package. Keep it with you as much as possible, in your pocket or purse during the day, under your pillow or on your night table when you sleep. Some Witches prefer to keep it tucked in a Work candle (when it's not lit, of course). Do this until the object itself appears. After that, you may keep the little string package in a holding place for magical objects. Some people reuse the same piece of string. I do not. I prefer to save the entire package as both a Power object and as an insurance that the object or being will not get lost again.

If the object of retrieval is a living being, say Words of Power to this effect:

So-and-so (*name being*) hereby returns home quickly and easily, according to Free Will and for the Good of All, and wherever he/she is he/she is divinely protected and perfectly safe, happy, healthy, alive, and well.

and/or:

According to Free Will and for the Good of All I hereby know where so-and-so is.

(This last statement is more for the comfort of the Witch than the missing being, who may want to stay absent for a while.)

Remember, when you are dealing with the free will of another being, the being may choose to stay away. The String Magic will aid him/her in returning if that is what he/ she wants. And of course you must modify the Words of Power so that you never even imply that a living being "belongs" to you!

This is a technique that may be successfully performed by non-Witches. If you want to aid others with String Magic, teach them these steps, and stand or sit nearby, speaking along with them, filling in their names where appropriate. You may prefer to do all the work silently in order to keep the Names of the Goddess and the God secret. However, allow the other person to write on the paper, physically use the string, and visualize as you chant. Don't be mysterious about it. Explain that the paper represents the lost object. The other, of course, then holds onto the paper and string until the object returns.

String Magic may sound deceptively simple, but you may be surprised at the amount of concentration and energy it can take.

CHAPTER 9

Psychic Help and Visualization

Familiars are entities that take on the role of companion and helper to a magical practitioner. The two most popular kinds of familiars are animal familiars and spirit familiars.

Animal Familiars

Animal familiars may be cats, dogs, rabbits, mice, toads, rats, or any animal that *volunteers* for the work. A familiar is not a pet even though to the untrained eye he or she may appear to be. A familiar is an equal from the animal realm, and it is a coworker for the Witch. A Witch may have many pets, but few familiars.

How do you recognize a familiar? Usually this is extremely obvious. The familiar is drawn to magical work in a non-intrusive way. A psychic link exists between the Witch and the animal, which is apparent to both and transcends speech—such as appearing frequently in each other's dreams and thoughts, and acting with total understanding of each other's needs. The familiar participates in as much of the magic as possible. Many familiars work in Circle. (Yes, even if it is *sleeping,* this is still participation! The key is non-intrusive presence.) It's always best to have the familiar present during scrying, tarot readings, spirit contact, and spell work. The animal energies add immeasurably to the Power drawn and used. Draw Down the Moon for your familiar as well as yourself (whether or not it is physically present) and include it in all your blessing work:

> And for (name familiar),
> The Goddess and The God give her/him
> Everything she/he needs and wants at all times including health, love, care, shelter, play, and understanding.

Never "train" your familiar by ordering it around, nor by giving it commands as some people do with their animals. Always talk to it as an equal. Allow your familiar to make its needs known to you, and be considerate of these needs, as you would be with any human friend. Invite your familiar to join in all the work. It may not always choose to join, so never try to force it.

If you ever have to leave your familiar in the care of another person—or even alone—for any given time, always explain everything to it first, and bless it by touching it with your pentagram. Actually, we now attach tiny, consecrated pentagrams to our familiars' collars. If your familiar is a cat, make sure to use a "break-away" cat collar, for safety. This will open if caught on something such as a tree branch. Try to leave your familiar in the care of another Witch.

Do not treat your familiar as you would a baby (unless, of course, it *is* a baby at this point). Do not "talk down" to it, nor wait on it paw and foot. Let your needs be known, too. Treat it as an equal.

If you do not have a familiar yet, you may send out a call for one. Let your call be similar to the Coven call. Remember that familiars also send out their calls, which explains the seemingly remarkable speed with which familiars and Witches often connect. Sometimes the familiar calls the Witch first. It is appropriate to specify the kind of animal you wish the familiar to be, but of course add "its equivalent or better form" because the familiar must agree with the form it takes or has already taken in linear time.

Those of us who have been Witches many times before have probably had the same familiars in many lifetimes. Some familiars who are particularly advanced are able to communicate psychically with their Witches in a kind of silent speech, which resembles spirit voices. In fact, when an animal familiar is not on this plane, the contact can continue in this manner, keeping the connection going until the animal reincarnates. This is usually a communication with an aspect of the animal's soul (see Aspects, chapter 13).

Most animals on this Earth plane do not live as long in linear time as humans (with the exception of some, such as tortoises and parrots, which can live longer). Thus a familiar may leave this plane at least once during the Witch's lifetime. Most often, both Witch and familiar want the animal to reincarnate and continue the relationship, and Words of Power are used to invite—never command—the familiar to return. Always allow the familiar to take the form in which it chooses to return. Familiars have their own karma to fulfill, which always meshes with the Witch's, but which includes many personal choices as well. For example, you may have had a cat in your life who returns as a dog, or a female animal who returns as a male.

Familiars seem to move easily between lifetimes and have much to teach us. Mine taught me that reincarnation is not necessarily linear, and that lifetimes, as we perceive them, can seem to overlap.

Thus it is quite possible that a familiar could return to its Witch as an adult animal, even though it might have left this plane—in linear time—just several weeks or months earlier.[1] Do not allow your personal perceptions of time or reincarnation to limit your familiar in any way. Always remember that the familiar is not only a helper, but also a teacher, and can help us transcend limiting ideas about the Universe, expand our perceptions, and develop our magic.

The most powerful force between familiar and Witch is always love.[2]

Spirit Contact

You may already be in touch with a spirit or spirits, but you may not be aware of this as such. Most spirit contacts in this culture are all too easily passed off as something else: a hunch, an intuition, inspiration, or creative thought. But there is a difference between your own inner thoughts and ideas, and the messages from the spirit realm. All it takes to tell the difference is concentration.

It takes, however, right-brain intuitive or "relational" concentration. This is concentration in a mode other than rational focus. Spirit contacts are traditionally referred to by non-Witches as

Personal Magic

"familiar spirits." By others, they are dubbed voices from the collective unconscious, spirit guides, archetypes, or alternate aspects of the self. The phenomenon of *channeled entities* also falls in this category. Some spirits themselves do not like to be called spirits, as they feel even that definition is too limited. When you get right down to it, it's a matter of semantics, because the World of Form has not yet come up with a non-limiting definition of Invisible Beings, nor for the unique form of communication that we can have with them deep inside our own minds.

In some New Age circles, this activity is now called *channeling* (in the old days, it used to be called *trance mediumship*). In this work, the person doing the channeling is believed to somehow leave her/his body, to let an *entity* come through to speak. Some entities have become quite famous and published books through their channellers. Who has actually written these books is not clear. Wise and helpful information has manifested in this manner, so some of this work is clearly reputable and honest. However, for private consultations or readings, when entities work through someone other than yourself—especially someone whom you don't personally know—there is sometimes (not always) too much latitude for errors. I recommend that each Witch does his/her own spirit contacting; a good method is during Aspect work.

There are many kinds of relationships to be had with beings in the Invisible World. Those who touch us and whom we touch can include:

1. Loved ones we knew in this life. These most often reach us in dreams, and such dreams should not be dismissed lightly.

2. Ancestors in linear time.

3. People we knew in other incarnations and who are not in Form during this lifetime.

4. Spokespeople from other cultures.

5. Animals, and even—

6. Yes, sorry to say—troublemakers.

Troublemakers rarely, if ever, have anything to do with a practicing Positive Witch, but if they should happen to intrude, they are easily banished, exorcised, or simply dismissed. To do this, one can hold up either the physical or invisible athame, call on Hecate or another appropriate Deity, and use a Release Spell to release them into their own good. The release spell can be as simple as this:

Short Release Spell
With Goddess and God Working for me and through
    me,
With divine protection
And According to Free Will and For the Good of All
I now release you (out of my life, out of this space)
Into your own Good
And so mote it be.

The kind of contact I recommend is one with coworkers or loving friends. The relationship should be equally beneficial to both spirit and Witch. One or more spirits are always available for sharing and exchanging information—for work, for comfort, for company, and for knowledge and growth. The Witch, of course, should be equally available to the spirit(s). These relationships are easy and natural, and being "on call" is automatic. Your own spirits are always completely compatible with your life, and you with theirs.

At this point "my" spirits advise me to add: *"All spirits are one."* They have said this before, and so have the spirits who work with my friends. They may manifest differently, speak (or send messages) in various styles and languages, appear in various guises, or demonstrate unique speech and message patterns and seem to have *different personalities*—but they are all One.

Knowing this, you may proceed to contact "your own" spirits.

The method I recommend is the following:

Sit in a quiet, darkened room, alone or with your familiar. Be totally relaxed. Light any candle(s) you choose. I use my work candle, Goddess candle, and/or God candle.

Hold a pen or pencil lightly in your hand, and have a notebook handy. It is advisable to keep a record of this work.

Say a Welcoming Blessing such as:

With Goddess and God working for and through me
I now welcome all who wish to participate in this work
for the Good of All and according to Free Will.
And so mote it be.

Put out your protection against any intruders, using your athame if you feel it is necessary. For protection, you may state your Alignments and call on your Deities.

For example:

Protection

The One Power is (*name your Deities*)

And I (*your name*) am (Deity) Incarnate

(Deity) Incarnate

and (Deity) Incarnate

I am perfectly Aligned with (Deity)

and perfectly Aligned with (Deity)

I am Priestess/Priest of (Deity)

I now call on (*name Deities*) for my perfect protection
   in this work—

Protection from any and all negative entities, thoughts,
   ideas, forms, essences, or anything or anyone
   other than Positive and life-affirming magic,
   energy, and contacts

According to free will

And for the good of all.

And so mote it be.

Then ask for the most perfect contact with the Invisible:

I now manifest the most perfect contact with the
   Invisible

I release everything and everyone negative

And welcome my loved ones as well as any other
   appropriate being in my life

For the most perfect positive and loving
   communication

According to free will

For the good of all

And so mote it be.

Of course, you may combine all of the previous, and make any variations you wish.

Sit and be still. Relax. Let your mind open.

Do not judge anything. When a word, a thought, an idea, a name, a feeling, an *anything* comes through—this is the beginning. Do not censor it, do not expect it to be different, do not expect any form. Make notes; either do this mentally or jot them down. Sit and be open; feel relaxed. Maintain the welcoming mood. If you happen to find yourself feeling frightened, do an extra blessing for protection, and reaffirm your Alignments.

Gradually, you will be able to distinguish a different "voice" than your own thoughts. It is difficult to describe in words, but to me it seems exactly like the feeling I have in the vicinity of my ears after someone has spoken to me, has told me something out loud. It's akin to the echo when your brain registers what you have just heard—although in this case, most likely, the words have not been spoken in the sense of physical speech.

One friend says that when the message comes through, it feels like a state of deep meditation. One says it feels like yoga relaxation exercises, and the message seems to come through her entire body, not just her ears (this from a dancer). Another actually *sees* her spirit friends, sort of like film projections on the ceilings and walls. The forms of Positive spirit contact are always different, and yet the feeling is the same. It's warm and friendly, loving and sharing. It's the touch between the worlds, and it's very powerful.

Most of us prefer to keep our records of these conversations in dialogue form. For example:

Me: Ok, do you have any further notes on this?

Them (spirits): Yes. Mention that we are not infallible, that we often only state our opinions. But we do have a certain advantage in maintaining the overview, and this we strive to make available to you all. Mention also that we may speak in several "voices" although at the initial contact, we try to manage just one. Because we only work for the good of all, and it must be mutually set up in this way, our communiqués are perfectly sane and beneficial.

Me: This sounds too defensive.

Them: No. It's an important point. The hearing of voices has been associated in your current culture with schizophrenia, and often rightly so. Disturbed spirits, you know, and no informed controls to bring them in. But the kind of contact between the worlds, which we recommend, is not nuts! Au contraire.

One more point: Spirit contact is a private affair.

Visualization

Simplistic, "pop" versions of visualization notwithstanding, when used as part of Witchcraft, visualization is a powerful technique for transformation and manifestation. It is a means of directing our lives in the World of Form. Visualization uses the Invisible World, where we ultimately have complete control. This control and direction is then transferred from the Invisible to the World of Form, helping us to achieve our desired results in our daily lives.

As with Words of Power, everybody does some amount of visualization without realizing it, and this *spontaneous visualiza-*

tion creates a large part of our life experiences. Spontaneous visualization can also occur in sleep dreams and daydreams. How many of these visions manifest in form has to do with how much power we give them.

To gain control over spontaneous visualization, learn to be watchful for images that seem to just pop into your head. Of course, if it is a favorable, positive image, bless it and allow it to manifest. For example, creative ideas occur in this way, and we can turn them into works of art.

If, however, you perceive an image that in any way is something you do not want, then you can intercede and change it with conscious visualization, starting with a simple Words of Power statement:

Words of Power to Transform a Visualization
By the One Power,
By (*name your Deities*)
Working for me and through me,
I now release this image and the situation it represents
And replace it with something much more life-
     affirmingly positive.
(*Then name and visualize the results you desire.*)
And so mote it be.

Using Visualization as a Tool for Manifestation

Begin by calling on your Deity Alignments and setting up your protection before embarking on this or any technique. Visualization is basically a ritual, and should be approached as one.

Words of Power to Begin a Visualization

There is One Power Which is Goddess and God
Which is (*name Deities*)
And I am (*name Deity*) incarnate
Perfectly Aligned with (name Deity)
I am Witch of (*name Deity*)
I am Priestess/Priest of (*name Deity*)
Therefore I call on my Deities now to work for me and
    through me
To create the perfect visualization of (*name goal*)
And to manifest this in my life,
According to Free Will
And for the Good of All
And so mote it be!

How to Visualize

Everybody has a personal style of visualization. Try to develop
your own. Here are some suggestions: After you state your
Words of Power and your goal:

Sit or lie comfortably.
Close your eyes.
Breathe deeply and evenly.
Relax your body.
Relax your mind; think of this process as easy and natural.
Affirm that this work will be pleasant.

1. Allow a picture to come before your eyes, very much like
   on a giant movie screen, or

2. Allow a scene to appear and surround you. In this case,
   you are now *in the picture*.

When visualizing something for yourself, it is usually best to be in the picture, because the goal is something that you desire to experience personally. It's more effective to put yourself into the scene by picturing the scene all around you.

Try to experience your visualizations as if you were living them, in a way that is realistic and complete. This way, you not only observe what is in the picture, you also hear it, smell it, and feel it with your senses. Place as many details in each picture as you can.

When doing visualization work for others—which is rather rare except for healing and must always be only at their request—there is usually no reason to put yourself in the picture. You can use the "movie screen" method, and you can be the observer.

Remember, you are the director of your own visualization as well as the principal actor. Therefore, you should endeavor to picture everything exactly as you want it to be—even if at first this seems impossible. You may wish to use the phrase, "*This, its equivalent, or better,*" in reference to your goal. Call on the Infinity of Solution:

What Not to Visualize

Never visualize *negative images:* If negative images do happen to come into your mind, this is an indication to do some transformation work to change the negative into the positive forms you wish.

Never visualize *manipulation* of others, ever! Manipulation is always a misunderstanding of magical work, and Positive Witches know better.

Allow for *the emotional component* of visualization. If you feel worried or frightened or otherwise in the grips of a limiting emotion, this could affect the results. So the thing to do is, not to *deny* the problem, but acknowledge it and transform it. Say Words of Power to release the emotional problem and replace it with a self-blessing along with the goals of your visualization.

For example:

> . . . I hereby release all doubt, worry, disbelief, fear, or any
> other block to the perfect manifestation of my goal,
> and I now replace all that with the infinity of Solution
> and (*re-state goal*) . . .

Then re-work the visualization with the desired effect.

Even non-sighted people can do effective visualization by experiencing the goal, for themselves, in whatever way feels effective and comfortable.

Remember, *visualization is perception*, and perception is always ultimately up to you.

Vision Guides

By visions, I mean images that are in one sense "imaginary" and yet in another context they may be considered totally real. They are symbols and pictures of the Power behind the symbol. Although many visions are, by nature, extremely personal and private, some visions may be shared—"seen"—by many. Here are two:

This image of the Goddess comes from a Renaissance depiction of Diana, which seems to have astrological significance, but actually it is a much older image. She stands on the Earth, Her feet touching the ground, but She is so huge that Her head reaches what we would now consider "airplane" level (about 30,000 feet). To summon up this beautiful vision, you may work Words of Power with full Alignments to send out a call, using as your goal:

> ... A perfect vision of You, Diana, Hecate, and Selene (or any Goddess),
> As The Big Goddess In The Sky.

Or you may send out a shorter version of a Call, something like this:

Dear Goddess,
As I am Your Priestess and Witch
In perfect Alignment with The God,
I hereby call on You—
According to Free Will
And for the Good of All,
Please manifest to me
As The Big Goddess In The Sky.
Thank You.
And so mote it be.

You will probably find that after you summon Her up a few times, She will appear to you when you feel you most need Her. You can work Words of Power directly to Her, even speak to Her, and don't be surprised if She answers. I have found that usually She answers with gestures. A wonderful image is for healing: ask Her to extend Her huge and powerful hand—even a finger—to touch the afflicted area. Thus, the image can take the form of Her finger coming through a window! And need I say this? This is not intended to replace medical care; but as with other healing work, is to be used as an adjunct to it.

This image of the Goddess is equally powerful against an unobstructed sky in nature or towering over city buildings. The expression on Her face may seem to change at various times, providing an oracle you may interpret to apply to whatever may be most on your mind. No matter how you choose to work with it, this image conveys a personal force field of comfort and love.

The Witch in The Forest

This is a vision that can be used as a personal oracle, or as a knowledge-quest. You can enter it in private meditation, indoors or out, with eyes closed and alone—or with eyes open in an appropriate spot in nature alone or with another Witch. Here are the guidelines, subject to your variations:

State Words of Power, with full Alignments, for protection and Divine guidance, for the most perfect vision of The Witch In The Forest, According to Free Will, and for the Good of All.

Picture yourself walking through a dense forest, deep in shadows. Picture a corner deep in the forest, underneath one particularly huge tree. Picture that a few feet away, in front of that tree, lies a fallen log, providing a very small clearing. There is no underbrush on the ground, just moss and a few rocks. This is a meeting place. Picture yourself approaching the log, and then sitting on it.

Stare at the tree trunk. Whisper "Sister," as a Call. Allow a dark shape to manifest against the tree. The shape is the size of a standing person. It is cloaked in black. Sit perfectly still, and stare at the shape until it turns into a Witch in a long black cloak. She may be holding a mirror, which probably will be black also.

When she has revealed herself to you fully, thank her for appearing, and tell her why you are there. If you have a question, ask it now. Her answer will either be spoken (silently), or it will appear in the mirror.

She may stay a while and share presence with you. When she indicates that she must go, thank her again, stand up, say

"Blessed Be," or a similar parting remark, and walk away from the log. If your eyes are closed, do not open them until you have walked out of the forest. If your eyes have been open, do not break your concentration until her image has faded completely.

Feel-o-vision

Well, that's what I call it—the directed use of *human emotion* to achieve a manifested goal. Actually, at the time of this writing, this technique doesn't yet have a recognizable name, is still surprisingly obscure, and is not even considered magic, never mind Witchcraft. But let us not get hung up with labels. When a method is used by a Witch for manifestation, it certainly seems to me that method becomes Witchcraft by means of the process. The medium is always the message.

Also, I believe that this is a truly ancient technique, because it is a missing link, an *adjunct* to visualization, ritual, and Words of Power. I suspect this controlled application of human emotion was automatically built into every magical process long ago. Today, we may not be aware of it, and have to study it separately, and then combine it with our other work.

Feel-o-vision. When I was a child in the late 1950s, and television was still new, there were all kinds of predictions and experiments for phenomena that would transform entertainment: smell-o-vision, 3-D movies, and yes, feel-o-vision. Unfortunately, these all fizzled out, with the exception of specialty theaters in theme parks, such as Disney World and Warner Brothers. They were grand ideas with silly results. Smell-o-vision featured scratch and sniff cards that were meant to illustrate turning points in the plot: the actors were walking through a field of flowers, and you scratched the first spot on the card and sniffed the flowers, then they sat in front of a fireplace and you scratched the smoke spot and sniffed that, etc. It was a great idea, but doomed. As for 3-D movies, everyone in the audience had to wear special cardboard glasses, and they didn't work. Now every few years someone tries to resurrect that cardboard technology, which still hasn't worked. And feel-o-vision: that had to do with the *seats!* The seats moved and jiggled and provided other sensations in a vain attempt to match the action on screen.

It is almost hilarious to note how our culture has sought meaning in simulations: Stage magicians pretending to do magic, pull rabbits out of hats, card tricks, rope tricks—illusion: Feel-o-vision of the most superficial kind. But the name stuck with me, and here is a really effective use for it—*the directed use of our own feelings as a source of power,* or feeling plus your vision.

Usually, our feelings seem autonomous. We may find that our feelings seem to be mostly reactions to events, people, and other stimuli. Our feelings are powerful, in that they can seem to overwhelm us. If our feelings are negative—such as anger, frustration, or depression—we may struggle with them because we don't want them to (this is perception) *take over.* If our feelings are positive—happy, excited, inspired—they still seem to exist in response to something that "made" us feel that way, and we seek whatever it was that "gave" us that feeling: exercise, religion, food, sex, romance, or drugs. What we often do not realize is that we *gave ourselves* the feelings—all of them. And now, it may seem as if the events or the people or whatever stimuli came along created our feelings. But get this: *Our feelings created* the events, the interactions with the people, actually the people themselves, or at least their presence in our lives—all of it. Our feelings create.

So here is this vast, untapped source of power. Or is it an impediment to the use of our personal power? Unfortunately, it is often an impediment.

For example, how can someone work magic for success in some endeavor if feeling discouraged, or magic for healing if feeling sick, or magic for happiness if feeling depressed, or magic for abundance if feeling lack? Well, with Words of Power, we can label the negative feeling, release it, and replace it with the desired goal. But to actually replace the *feeling itself*—with a more positive and appropriate one—that is often a speedier and more effective technique. The reason? The feeling creates a corresponding image of itself.

To be simplistic: A happy feeling creates happy circumstances. A wealthy feeling creates wealth and abundance. A feeling of loss can create further loss. This is the reason that when a person experiences the death of a loved one, other losses often occur on the physical plane—loss of money, of friendships, or of belongings. If a person feels depressed, sad things just seem to happen.

It really isn't quite so simple, because other factors are at play, such as karmic ones. For example, a person could be feeling depressed and lonely, and suddenly friends and loved ones could come along and provide love and comfort to transform that negative feeling. However, usually if one feels depressed and lonely, one would find oneself increasingly alone and surrounded by sad circumstances—unless and until that person does something to change the pattern. The pattern can always be changed, because we created it in the first place. Sometimes one creates a change that appears to come from outside the self (such as the previously mentioned friends). But according to this theory, all changes come from within the self. The idea that outside events cause anything at all in our lives is an illusion. *We cause the event.* And surprisingly often, we cause the event by means of our feelings. The event echoes and demonstrates our feelings, just as it demonstrates our beliefs and ideas.

Feelings are fabulous tools. Here's how to use them:

1. First of all, be aware of what they create: actual circumstances in our lives.
2. Next, be aware that you can control and direct them.

Simply put, the easiest way to use your feelings is to feel the way you believe you would feel, the way you really want to feel, when your goal has already been accomplished—that is the goal of your magic. In other words, experience and feel the fulfillment of your goal, even before it manifests in the World of Form. Of course, non-Witches can use this technique, too, without the added techniques of magic. But because we are Witches, I recommend that you add the feeling you want, right along with your chosen magic—ritual, Words of Power, visualization, whatever.

Sometimes it may seem difficult or even impossible to create a feeling before you actually experience the end result. Sometimes you might even experience a negative feeling that won't budge. Or a negative one that goes away, and then seems to bounce right back again. So of course you release the negative and replace it with your feeling of choice, as we said. The best way to do this is tried and true Words of Power. But what if even that seems difficult?

Ideally, magic should not be difficult.

There are techniques for mastering your feelings, so that they become available for your use. Of course this is not in any way a recommendation to hide or submerge your true feelings. These techniques are to be used after you acknowledge your feelings, honor them, and then choose to release their grip on your future progress. In other words, wallowing is definitely not recommended, however compelling.

For Control of General Feelings

Acknowledge and experience the unwanted feeling for as long or as short a time as seems minimally necessary, and then completely turn your attention to something else. Think about a number of pleasant things, until you choose one that makes you feel generally good. If there are several effective ideas, make a list and use them as needed. The point is to switch over to feeling back in control, comfortable, and happy. This should be your starting point for the work, because this is approximately how you want your goal to feel. It really doesn't matter what the subject is; the feeling is what matters. So if I feel worried or afraid of something, I acknowledge that for just long enough to know what that feels like, and then I switch over to thinking about my kittens—and how good their silly cavorting makes me feel.

Well that's what works for me. I know at first glance this could be interpreted as superficial or naive. But who cares! This is a technique that actually *works*, doesn't hurt, and always helps. Instead of kittens, you could use a Mozart opera, a Tchaikovsky ballet, a Shakespeare sonnet, the Gettysburg Address, or anything else that *reliably* makes you feel good. A popular choice is to select one positive attribute of yourself—

and perceive *that*. Another technique is to focus on a different positive attribute of yourself each day—for a month! That would be thirty positive attributes. These are all tools to enhance the effectiveness of your magic.

This process of switching the subject matter is a lot like sense-memory techniques used by actors. A famous actress once disclosed that when she needed tears for a tragic scene, she thought about her dog dying, and her tears were convincing and genuinely wet—because they were real. Well, this works the same way—except in this case, please think about your dog being healthy and happy and doing something that brings you joy, such as catching a frisbee or peeing in the right place.

For Control of Full-Time Feelings

Just as we do well to watch our words even when we are off-duty from working magic, and control negative statements by taking them out of the Law (of Cause and Effect) or adding "No harmful power, turn this to good"—so can we watch our feelings and control them as well. Non-Witches can just watch their feelings and switch them, as described previously. We Witches can add "No harmful power; turn this feeling to good." And then switch them.

Specific Feelings

Another effective technique is to relive an occasion that made you feel specifically the way you want your goal to make you feel. If you are working magic for abundance, relive the way you felt when you got your first allowance, or your first job, if these are appropriate examples. (Otherwise, pick another one.) If you are working magic for healing, feel the way you felt at your most athletic and strong. If it is magic for love, feel the way you felt when you were the most loved, even if that love was in your childhood, from your mother—or from your dog! It doesn't matter what you use as your sense memory to relive your feeling. Just get the feeling, harness it, and send it out with your magic. If you think that the feeling source is inappropriate for your current goal— even though its intensity and vibration was correct—you can always add an adjustment to your Words of Power:

> I now feel as loved as I did the first time Spot licked
> my face, only this time, the feeling comes from a
> human love relationship, licking not necessary.

Just be careful when you choose to work with a sense-memory feeling: when you wish to relive something, *only relive that which is positive.* If other problems seem to be mixed in to the memory, let it go, and choose something else.

Expanded Goals

The proponents of working with feelings are generally devoted to the Infinity of Solution—even if not by that name. Because limitation is a feeling, they encourage their students to seek and feel unlimited goals. I agree.

Feel-o-vision—or whatever we choose to call it—may seem difficult at first, but it is not really difficult, just different. It presents an entirely new context for dealing with life, and like most magic, may seem impossible at first. As we practice it, we grow comfortable with working in this way, and the results help us to transcend our initial disbelief. I suspect that time will reveal infinite possibilities in working with the power of feelings.

CHAPTER 10

Contacting the Departed

There are myriad ways to communicate with those who have left this plane and for them to contact us. Dreams, of course, are tried, true, and traditional avenues for those on the other side to reach us. Even if the dream imagery can become a bit confused, the emotional reality of the contact is unmistakable, and dreams can be an excellent way of obtaining messages as well as solid comfort from loved ones who have moved on.

Ouija boards can be helpful, if cumbersome, instruments for communication. Of course, Words of Power are essential for setting up the contact accurately and safely. Psychic or "spiritual" readers and mediums can be accurate, but often provide inappropriate contacts for the Witch. This is due to the built-in lack of privacy because of a third party (the reader), and also due to the usually non-Wiccan religious or spiritual persuasion of the psychic. But some psychics are wonderful, and so are their books.[1]

Departed loved ones may appear spontaneously in any number of manifestations—from voices and images to symbols in daily life. A book could fall open to a certain passage, a meaningful musical phrase could be heard on the radio, a beloved object could fall off a shelf. I think it must be hard work for such loved ones to make themselves known to us, unless we are extraordinarily receptive. And even then, the contact might be sadly one-sided. How are *we* to contact *them* when we need them, or simply to let them know we want to keep in touch? I look forward to the day when science or technology—or someone or something—can provide an instrument of communication that has at least one end as a physical object in the World of Form. I have heard of experiments with high-tech tape recorders played at unusual speeds or frequencies, and specially devised cameras and electrical devices. Not surprisingly, these devices are often used to prove that ghosts exist, rather than contact our loved ones. But none of these have either convinced skeptics or helped serious seekers. Perhaps it is inappropriate for us to use any physical means to contact departed loved ones at this time, instead of simply relying on our own sincere thoughts and feelings.

A dear friend—a writer who wishes to remain anonymous—taught me a meditation technique that is the best form of spirit contact I've heard of, to date. She says she thought everyone knew how to do it. I didn't. It's remarkably simple. However, it only works when, and if, both parties want it. If your loved one does not wish to communicate at any particular time, this does not necessarily have any negative meaning. Contact simply may not be appropriate, for any number of reasons.

This method is based on the theory that when beings leave this plane they reach a point in their development where they each can literally create their own environment and personal appearance. In that realm, they can somehow manifest exactly where they want to be and how they wish to look. They may share their surroundings with others, or they may choose to stay alone, at least during the time of contact with us.

With this in mind, it is important, before you begin, to rid yourself of all preconceptions and expectations of how you think your loved one will look or what kind of environment he/she will have chosen. Actually, they often appear much as we've known them—perhaps a bit younger or healthier—but their chosen surroundings may be a complete surprise to us.

Most often, it's best to do this meditation in private, in a comfortable space, possibly with dim lighting. *No distractions.* A candle is optional.

Work Words of Power first, for a safe, positive, clear, and enjoyable communication with your loved one (*state name*) according to Free Will and for the Good of All.

Try something such as:

Words of Power for Communication
With a Departed Loved One
(*state Alignments, then add*):
With the One Power
Which is Goddess and God Working for and through
    me
I hereby manifest the perfect communication with
(*name loved one*) according to free will and for the good
    of all only.

If it is not right for us to communicate now
Then I manifest all the information I need to under-
    stand this.
If it is correct for us to communicate now
The Goddess and God work through both of us
For our meeting in perfect safety, joy, and love
And so mote it be.

Close your eyes, lean back or lie down, and meditate upon your loved one's voice, face, and/or name. Perhaps you will hear him/her call your name. Listen, be open, and clear your mind of all else. Do not try to force anything. A sound or image will present itself.

Whatever the image is, follow it. You may see a path, road, or street. You might even see a messenger of some sort. Again, follow.

Follow until you come to a house or other living area. Remember: No preconceptions! Do not try to visualize the environment where your loved one will be staying. Let it reveal. Go into the area.

Your loved one will be there. It's as simple as that. Have a beautiful visit. Get all the information he/she wants to tell you. Ask questions and listen for the answers. If necessary, you both may begin to heal the relationship in a way you might not have been able to on this plane. You will probably find your loved one's attitudes and philosophies somewhat changed. Know that this is the first of many visits, should you both choose, so there's no need to try to cram everything in. Keep it relaxed. You may feel quite emotional at first. No blame; eventually you will both adjust. If there are any problems, do Words of Power together.

You will know when the visit should end. Do not cling or hold on to either your loved one or the vision. Because I am a writer, I find it helpful to make notes afterward, but this is really not necessary. You will remember what's important. The fact that you were able to do this, even once, indicates that you both have all of eternity to meet again, together, should you both choose.

CHAPTER 11

Protection

Psychic Attack

Without the phenomenon of psychic attack, there would probably be no horror movies, or at least pitifully few. Horror movies are the ritualistic means our culture uses to release that which people find most frightening—and for which modern civilization has provided no practical explanations or guidelines. Although not always properly defined, psychic attack usually seems to show up as that evil unseen force that manifests where you least expect it, with no warning, often for no apparent reason, except to cause harm—and all of this is usually in one's own home. Ooooh, that's scary!

The uninitiated usually turn either to science or traditional religion to combat psychic attack. Science combats psychic attack by essentially saying it doesn't really exist, except in the mind. The Judeo-Christian tradition combats it by employing experts (special priests, ministers, or rabbis) who label the attack the work of the devil or evil demons, and ritually ask God to fight off, cast out, and generally vanquish these ungodly beings. Actually this vanquishing activity takes place only in the more orthodox religious branches, because the more modern branches of Judaism and Christianity also say that psychic attack doesn't really exist, or that it's all in the mind of the beholder.

An interesting blend of religion and science—or pseudo-science—is the phenomenon of "ghost-busters:" specialists who use technological equipment to track, measure, and generally deal with paranormal activity.

Jewish and Christian religious beliefs are relatively new (approximately 4,000 and 2,000 years old, respectively) compared to Witchcraft and other Pagan religions. In general, Judeo-Christian tradition posits a separation of good and evil, God and devil or demons. In this view, combating psychic attack is really considered a kind of warfare. This can be seen as an expression of the Judeo-Christian worldview of good and evil, which did not exist 4,000 years ago.

In Witchcraft, there is no conceptual separation of Deity vs. devil. The Goddess and the God include all of creation in their dominion. So anything—even something as awful as psychic attack (and its perpetrators)—still remains under the jurisdiction, so to speak, of our own Deities. Nothing can be blamed on some nefarious enemy, such as the devil. Nor do we believe we have to pit our own Deities against any other powerful, unusually horrendous being—and then have to worry about who is going to win. Also, we don't have to hire any expert middleman to get rid of a psychic attack for us in the name of our Deity (although sometimes we may want the help of other Witches).

We believe, as our Alignments affirm, that each one of us is a perfect manifestation of The Goddess and The God. In this context, our own Power is seen as equal to the Power of whomever might have sent the attack. Also, because a misuse of this Power could have caused the attack—then the correct use of this Power can end the attack. The Universal Power is basically neutral; the way in which it is used is what makes it seem to be good or evil.

Consequently, the way that Witches traditionally deal with evil is not to try to destroy it, but to *transform* it. Negative energy is transformed to Positive energy. This is a very important process: Negative (life-denying) into Positive (life-affirming). In Positive Witchcraft, this is the way exorcisms are performed, the way healings are performed, and the way psychic attacks are repelled.

Seen in this comforting context, the phenomenon of psychic attack usually seems less frightening to Witches than to the rest of the population.

I wrote this a few years ago, and now looking at it, I wonder, *What was I thinking?* Psychic attack can still be thoroughly scary, even for a Witch. So we should never allow ourselves to be smug or unprepared, because such an attitude is not much better than the modern scientific view that denies the very existence of psychic attack. In fact, a source of the apparent power of any psychic attack is its ability to sneak up unobtrusively on a person who is unaware. It can look like plenty of other "natural" phenomena, all the while wearing down the victim's resistance until the inevitable fear sets in, and then the attack can feed off that.

What is psychic attack? It can take so many forms that an accurate definition might be elusive; but we can describe it in this way:

Psychic attack comes through the Invisible Realm. It may even be sent by invisible beings, or it may be sent by incarnate beings on this Earth Plane. It may be sent by ordinary people thinking negative thoughts powered by intense negative emotions. Or it may be sent by practitioners of any number of negative traditions, such as Satanism. It might totally backfire—for example, by means of the Threefold Law, if one has directed negative work at another person. Thus, a psychic attack can be sent accidentally or on purpose, by amateurs or by "professionals." In any case, it is always initiated by negative energy.

Most often, a psychic attack manifests in the World of Form, where it can take many forms. Some forms might resemble negative hauntings, such as the phenomena of unpleasant smells or sounds. Or the attack could manifest as an illness, an apparent accident, severe depression, or a pervasive feeling of malaise. Some forms of mental illness could actually be the result of psychic attack. Or the attack could manifest as an uncharacteristic emotion seeming to take over the victim, such as irrational anger, or any other emotion that could possibly harm others, and endanger the victim's relationships.

A traditional form of psychic attack could be an invasion of vermin: unwanted and unpleasant insects, rats, or worms (definitely not the garden-friendly variety.) Other forms could manifest as a fire or flood of mysterious origins, usually in a limited area.

How do you tell the difference between a psychic attack and any of these occurrences happening by natural causes? The psychic attack is *unusual;* it seems to come out of nowhere, and there is a mood of strangeness about it, for those who are sensitive and attuned enough to notice. Personal karma—the sustained sequences of cause and effect—are usually quite clear to the thoughtful Witch. Even misfortunes can be clearly understood, with close examination, meditation, and the use of oracles. But psychic attack does not fall under any of the usual karmic categories; it literally seems to come mysteriously from "outside" the Witch's own life.

Another telltale characteristic is that, while virtually any problem can be solved by Words of Power work, a problem caused by psychic attack often will not go away permanently (until it is properly diagnosed). Instead, it may seem to remanifest, perhaps in various forms. These manifestations may be stripped of all serious negative power and definitely "watered down" by Words of Power work. Yet if they continue to remanifest, that means the root cause is probably not solved.

Another characteristic is that whatever form a psychic attack takes, it feeds on feelings of vulnerability and fear.

In some traditions, people who believe in the power of psychic attack (or Voodoo or Obeiah, or whatever the local name may be) can sicken and die. The cause is a combination of their own fear, their own feelings of vulnerability, and the negativity of the attack itself. Such attacks are often otherwise so ineffectual that without belief in the power of this particular negative tradition and the attendant emotional terror—often no effect at all will be felt. Thus we hear reports about missionaries, anthropologists, and others outside a given community who remain untouched by the same evil technique that has been known to kill true believers. Outsiders to such traditions have often concluded two erroneous beliefs about such attacks:

1. The victim must be consciously aware of the attack in order to feel its effects, and then simply falls prey to some sort of self-hypnosis. This is untrue, because the attack is by definition psychic. One would be just as likely to be aware of it psychically as if one were told about it. And negative self-hypnosis is not what lends such an attack its power; the attack can carry actual negative power with it (although usually very little). *But fear is the doorway through which the attack can enter a person's life.* When fearing such an attack, a person consequently relinquishes all personal Power, which could, if used properly, actually repel the attack.

2. Psychic attacks are a form of Witchcraft and that the specialists in sending these attacks are "Witch doctors." This is a semantic difficulty, due to a tendency on the part of this culture to label all forms of magical work—often negative—as Witchcraft. A careful respect for the language of other traditions would yield a whole spectrum of words meaning different kinds of magic and magical practitioners. A good analogy: The Inuit (Eskimo) people have numerous words for different kinds of snow, but they all translate into English as simply snow.

How to Deal With Psychic Attack

Actually, the best approach is to deal with it very much like an attack of a virus or the flu. These are minor ailments that can seem to sneak up on us, but they are easily dealt with, if caught early. We all have been able, on occasion, to stop a cold at its beginning, and get rid of it before it actually starts. And even if it does start—a cold or flu can be treated in a variety of effective ways—from hot tea, to traditional over-the-counter medication, to herbal remedies, to the latest antibiotics.

The best attitude to have is a realistic one. Neither fear nor deny the possibility of psychic attack. Just be aware that it could possibly happen; but also be aware that it's really nothing to be afraid of, because you are in control of your own life, and you can control potential attacks in two ways:

1. You can prevent them from occurring, just like colds and flu.
2. You can get rid of them even if they should occur—just like pesky bugs.

Prevention

Just as you can protect yourself from flu in cold weather by dressing and resting properly as a matter of course, so you can protect yourself from psychic attack by using Words of Power for divine protection as a matter of course. Notice, especially, if you feel something unpleasant afoot, such as reports of "ill will" or jealousy from others; but please, no paranoia here! Ideally, you strengthen your body against most viruses or flu by building up your immune system and general constitution—with good nutrition, proper vitamins and minerals, and the right balance of exercise and rest. So you should nourish and build up your psyche by frequent Goddess/God Alignments and the practice of Positive Magic and Positive Witchcraft only. The wearing of consecrated Craft jewelry, such as a pentagram, also serves as powerful protection.

An absolutely foolproof way to invite a psychic attack is to launch one on another person or being; because everything, as we know, returns to the sender. Also remember, the more good you do for others (never at the expense of yourself, of course, never as a martyr, and always according to Free Will and for the Good of All), the more positive feedback will return to you by the Threefold Law. All of the holiday celebrations, all the Moon work, all attunement with the Universal forces of nature—all the work of the Positive Witch, in other words—strengthens the soul in the Invisible World, and helps build up immunity to psychic attack.

Early Warnings and Symptoms

If you're alert to the first sneeze or sniffle, it's easier to get rid of a slight cold than a full-blown attack of flu—so it's also much easier to get rid of a psychic attack when it first manifests as a mere annoyance before it turns into something more unsavory (which is most often, although not always, the case). In both circumstances, *avoid denial*. To assume that early symptoms are really nothing, to avoid noticing a problem when it's still small, or to think that if you ignore something you don't like, it will go away—these are all unrealistic and potentially dangerous attitudes. This does not mean you should become a psychic hypochondriac or become worried or frightened; as I said earlier, we don't want to create an atmosphere of vulnerability. We want, instead, to assert and draw upon our own Power, and take responsibility for our own well being, even in small ways. After all, if you feel slight flu symptoms, it certainly doesn't hurt to take extra vitamin C, get extra rest, and carry an extra sweater. Well, in the presence of small, vague, mysterious manifestations, it also wouldn't hurt to repeat extra Alignments, Words of Power specifically for protection, and visualize a Protective Shield around oneself and one's loved ones. In either case, you can nip a potential problem right in the bud.

Diagnosis

Any Witch who is experiencing a problem that does not yield directly to Words of Power work, should then work Words of Power to reveal the exact nature of the problem—specifically whether it has been caused by psychic attack. The oracles should also be used—tarot cards, *The I Ching*, and pendulum—to help figure things out. Spirit guides may also be consulted. It's of ten a good idea to consult other Witches.

It is helpful, but not necessary, to know where the attack is coming from.

Words of Power for Diagnosis of Psychic Attack
(*state alignments, then add*):
With the One Power
Which is Goddess and God Working for me and
    through me
I now reveal the exact nature of what seems to be a
    problem
I now understand clearly if there is a psychic attack
    involved

Or whatever else the cause is
I understand everything I need to know
In order to release it completely
In all time and all space
All according to Free Will and for the Good of All
In perfect safety and divine protection for my loved
    ones and myself
(then add the Words of Power Statement for Repelling
    a Psychic Attack, which follows).

Treatment

Words of Power are the cure. They can be combined with ritual if you prefer. Goddess and God Alignments are the antidote. Rest and special consideration ("being good to yourself") comprise the aftercare. Wearing Craft jewelry, carrying consecrated crystals, repeating Alignments frequently, visualizing the Protective Shield, consulting the oracles regularly—these constitute prevention of any further attack.

How the Treatment Works

The Words of Power in effect, dissipate the psychic attack and may even bounce it right back to its sender. This process transforms the surrounding energies in the former victim's life from negative to positive. In this holistic approach, there is no feeling of a battle, and the basic Oneness of all life is reaffirmed.

Because the energy of the Universe may be seen as neutral, the perpetrator who initiated the attack worked (either consciously or unconsciously) to color this neutral energy as negative. By dealing directly with the energy at its basic level (which is what the Words of Power work does), the Witch transforms all the energy in the afflicted area back to positive. Any energy which for any reason is compelled to remain negative will be returned to sender.

Remember, in the Wiccan view, *everything*, both positive and negative, is ruled by our Deities. There is no separation or division in the Universal scheme; everything is linked. Human perception may have decreed that the Universe is a battleground of good versus evil, but this is perception only. As we adjust our perception back to the holistic Pagan view, we can see that *there is no evil power to combat*. There is simply neutral energy, once colored negative, now to be redefined. The positive Power the Witch uses to accomplish this is no less powerful than the negative Power the perpetrator drew upon. In fact, the use of the positive Power is stronger, because it is not burdened with the trappings of the negative, which is ultimately self-destructive. As *The I Ching* explains:

> ... The dark power ... in the end ... perishes of its own
> darkness, for evil must itself fall at the very moment
> when it has wholly overcome the good, and thus con-
> sumed the energy to which it owed its duration.

> —*The I Ching*, Hexagram 36
> Six at the top

And just as a characteristic of negative Power is to destroy itself, so a characteristic of positive Power is to renew itself.

I consider this work to be primarily Hecate's domain. She rules the shadows, the areas comprising death, rebirth, transformation, and justice. All of this comes into play in dealing with a psychic attack.

Suggested Procedure for Repelling a Psychic Attack

When composing the appropriate Words of Power, it's important to be as specific as possible. The arrow has to hit the target.

Your emotional atmosphere should be as calm as possible. No anger! Instead, use calm clarity. Concentrate on the Words of Power work, *not on the person or entity who sent the attack.* Release any fear; instead, feel confidence in your Deities and your relationship to Them. Concentrate on the Power of your Alignments rather than on the apparent Power of the attack. If you choose, you may use a Hecate cord (unless it's Her time, the Waning or Dark of the Moon). Use a Work Candle, or better yet, use all your candles. Use your athame first, holding it upright during this work and then pointing it opposite you during the closure. Draw a pentagram in the air over the candles at some point during the work.

Another effective method is to stand outdoors, in the wind. Face the direction the wind is blowing toward—in other words, let the wind be at your back. Use your athame. A candle may not stay lit, unless you place it in a tall container. Otherwise, use your Invisible candles. Say your Words of Power into the wind, and let it blow them away from you.

Words of Power for Repelling a Psychic Attack
(*State Alignments, then add:*)
By the One Power, The Goddess and God,

Working for me and through me,
I (*name*) am divinely protected and perfectly safe,
My loved ones are all divinely protected and perfectly
    safe,
According to Free Will and for the Good of All
In all time and all space,
I hereby release
All cause, all manifestation, all form, and all essence
Of everything and anything negative—
Specifically having to do with any psychic attack,
I specifically release all cause all effect, manifestation,
    form, or essence of anything having to do with
    (*name symptoms, if any*)—
All of this and anything else negative, named or
    unnamed,
Is dissolved and released and turned to good, in my life
    and the lives of my loved ones,
In the Names of my Deities.
In the Name of You, Diana, Hecate, Selene,
    Kernunnos, and Pan (*or Deities of your choice*),
All psychic attack is now gone,
And I am free;
And so mote it be!

One final note of caution about "contagion:" Don't be too eager to do the job of repelling psychic attack for another person. If you absolutely must do this, please consult your oracles first, and use the help of your coven, or at least several other Witches who really want to help. And always start with self-protection of each Witch.

Housecleaning

Of course this means *psychic* housecleaning! But it's not meant only for houses; this is also cleaning of any space where a Witch will reside, such as a hotel room or a guestroom.

This work is appropriate any time you are going to spend even one night in a place. It is not necessary if you are using the space for a brief period of time—say, taking a nap on a friend's couch. But it would be a good idea to use it if you're planning to hold meetings or workshops, or if you are opening a store, or other venture. Other appropriate subjects for this work: used cars and trucks, boats, tents, sleeping bags, used furniture, and clothing that belonged to someone else—no matter who it was! Sleeping in a space overnight is not the only criteria. You can use your judgment, assessing the time to be spent in a given space, the purpose of the space's use, and of course the history and vibrations of the space itself. Just be sure that the psychic housecleaning is performed entirely in private; no outsiders should watch. Other Witches can assist, if desired.

If you haven't performed this or a similar ritual in your own home, I highly recommend that you do so. Traditionally, this work has been used in rooms where negative events have occurred and unpleasant vibrations may still linger. But the purpose is not merely to release negatives, although of course this is always an effective result. The purpose is to consecrate the space for you and your loved ones to be safe, comfortable, and happy all the time you are there.

If it turns out that indeed the space has had a negative history, or has somehow been tainted by negative energies, then this work may have to be performed several times, over several weeks, months, or even years. Just like dust, "bad vibes" have to be regularly cleaned out. But happily (and unlike dust), once they are truly out, they are gone for good.

Cleaning Instructions
Use a candle and, if you wish, your athame. I would use either a Work or Goddess candle, but the choice is yours. Starting at the door or entrance, with candle lit—walk slowly clockwise, through the house, through each room, pausing at each door and window and moving the candle across it. Also, pentagram each window and door with your athame or pointing your (Goddess ringed) finger. Proceed room-by-room, floor-by-floor, spiraling clockwise. If you cannot or do not wish to enter a room—or even a whole floor, such as a cellar or attic—then stand at the entrance, or at a staircase, and mentally traverse the space clockwise, mentally covering each window and door. All the while, chant Words of Power according to this guide, with whatever changes you wish.

> **Suggested Words of Power for Housecleaning**
> (*State Alignments, then add:*)
> By the One Power, Goddess and God working for and
>   through me,
> I hereby consecrate this space
> To The Goddess and The God,
> According to Free Will,
> And for the Good of All,
> I hereby release,

In all time and all space,
Any negative cause, effect, manifestation, form, or
    essence,
Any negative event, thought, energy, idea, or vibration,
And transform it to
And replace it with
Only positive, joyous good
In keeping with the Universal harmonies
Of The Goddess and The God.
This space is divinely protected.
This space is perfectly safe.
Nothing and no one can enter this space
Unless I (or my loved ones) allow them to.
This space is sacred Consecrated and dedicated to
    positive living
For myself and my loved ones
And for the work of Positive Magic and Positive
    Witchcraft only.
No harm can come to this space, or anyone in it.
(*As you pentagram each door and window*):
Only good can enter here
No negatives can enter
All harm is sealed out
(*When you are back at entry point, conclude*):
Love lives here, Health lives here, Abundance lives
    here, Joy lives here,
(*Name self and loved ones*) live (or work/etc.) here
We claim this space for ourselves, for the mutual good
And so mote it be!

History and Mystery

If you are reading this Book of Shadows, you probably have a pretty good idea of the basic history of Witchcraft in Western Europe. The story goes something like this:

Before the introduction of Christianity, all of Europe was Goddess-worshipping and Pagan. Life depended on the Earth. Religion was totally centered on the Earth, and Witches were an important part of the mix.

From approximately 1300 to 1500, a terrible persecution descended on Europe—targeting Pagans, Witches, women (old ugly women and beautiful young women), and also Wizards, midwives, and surgeons. And oh, yes, homosexuals. Anyone else who was believed to have anything to do with a Witch or Pagan was also targeted. Corruption, genocide, hypocrisy, widespread persecution, the whole holocaustal package lasted 300 years, a time known even to non-Witches as The Dark Ages. The reasons were political, as rulers of every little kingdom and duchy converted to the new religion of Christianity, and made waste of anyone who did not do the same. To complicate things, the Crusaders returned from their pillaging travels with stories about something they had seen in the mysterious East: statues of evil gods with horns. The Pagan Horned God in Europe bore superficial resemblance—therefore the concept of the anti-Christian devil was born. All non-Christians were accused of being this devil's worshippers. Witchcraft in particular was decreed to be the precise opposite of the Church.

Not even cats were spared from wholesale slaughter. Thus, in one of the supreme ironies of this darkest of times, with the murder of virtually all the cats in Europe, the Bubonic Plague raged unchecked, for the simple reason that there were no cats left to control the rats that carried the Black Death. The reason for burning millions of cats? Well, everyone knew they were really Witches in disguise, and burning Witches was de rigeur. It was a holy act, a war against the devil, and besides, for every accused Witch who was murdered, there was property to be confiscated. All in then the name of God.

Today with the luxury of enlightened hindsight, some modern Witches debate about exactly how many of our wretched number were actually killed in Europe. We know the collateral damage added obscene numbers—Witches' entire families, for example, and neighbors. At least one town in Germany was left with no women alive. We know that many if not most of the victims weren't even Witches, just guilty by means of accusation. The previously accepted number of people killed was 9 million. Well, the time period extended past several hundred years, so generations were involved and that high estimate seemed to make sense until recently. Now, some scholarly Witches say that number is impossible; there weren't even that many people in Europe over that time period, never mind Witches.

Does it matter?

An entire religion was virtually stamped out. The sacred Books of Shadows were all burned, the Bubonic Plague destroyed whole communities. The Inquisition brought barbaric persecution to new and horrific levels. The theological sanctity of women was stamped out. The Goddess and all She stands for was gone—or at least absent from society for almost a millennium. To this day, the Inquisitors' definition of Witchcraft is still prevalent: The *Malleus Malificarum*, one of the first handful of books ever published, fabricated Witchcraft as the religion of Satan. Today's encyclopedias and dictionaries still carry this lie. So magic has effectively been absented from our culture since roughly the 14th century.

Does it matter how many people were killed? More important is *why* they were killed.

I think these are the questions to ponder: If Witches were targeted—even along with innocent bystanders—how and why did they allow their own destruction? Where was the power of magic when we needed it?

I used to say that the only explanation I could think of was the tragic vulnerability of a sort of beatific denial. Not unlike the Jews in Nazi Germany, the welcoming Aztecs, and the trusting Native American tribes—all groups with intense spirituality and Divine purpose, and all destroyed. If it wasn't denial, and turning the other cheek, what message could we glean from the unspeakable destruction of each powerfully spiritual religious group? Were their Deities so helpless, was their devotion so powerless, that it failed them totally?

Now I think it could have been something else. I believe that along with the physical attacks came the more secret, hidden yet powerful psychic attacks. Historians note in passing that in the vanquished Nazi bunkers were found bodies of robed Eastern, possibly Tibetan, Shamans: Some sort of exotic advisors. Many theories abound about the Nazis' inner sanctum as a devilish cabal, even theories about racial superiority had a religious tinge, hinting at more secret ideologies and practices.

My new theory is that every conquering group attacks first on the psychic level. Not on every battlefield, although we hear of more than one clergyman blessing the troops. I refer to specific events—wholesale destruction of entire racial groups, karmic groups bound together by a religious tie. The most effective way would be to pray to whatever power seemed appropriate to join in the fray and ask it to erode the spiritual fiber from within. And as mentioned earlier, the primary if not only power of psychic attack is when it is unknown, unnoticed, and therefore not defended against.

Knowing this, Witches can repeat the recent slogan, "Never again The Burning Time!"

Protective Shields

Any time you want an extra measure of protection and safety for yourself or a loved one, visualize the following: A clear, silver-tinted, egg-shaped shield, completely surrounding yourself or the other person. This shield is invisible to others, but, of course, they will sense its presence. Visualize this frequently, during the course of time you wish to invoke it (yes, if you like, it can be used daily, or even all the time). This is particularly handy for a child going off to school or camp, for yourself during a dentist or doctor visit, for a loved one in a hospital or on a plane, a familiar at the vet, or anyone during various excursions and trips. It doesn't have to be a particularly dangerous mission in order to invoke this shield—or it can be. So if you or a loved one are off on an experimental space shuttle mission or diving 20,000 leagues under the sea, I would say this shield is a requirement. You can place a pentagram on the shield, for an extra dose of Positive Witchcraft Power. As you visualize it, use the following (or your variation):

Words of Power for Creating a Protective Shield
(*State Alignments, then add:*)
The One Power Working for and through me,
Hereby manifests and creates The invisible Protective
  Shield
Of The Goddess (and of the God)
According to Free Will,
And for the Good of All,
Nothing and no one
Can negatively penetrate
This Shield.
(*Name*) is now impervious to all harm,
I (*he, she*) am (*is*) now divinely protected,
And perfectly safe,
In all time and all space,
And so mote it be!

The Witches' Bottle

This is a powerful method of protection, taught to me by Selena Fox. The Witches' Bottle is primarily designed for protection of a place, but it may be used for protection of individuals also— just use a smaller bottle that can be carried around, such as a baby food jar.

The Witches' Bottle is traditionally buried in the earth. If you live in an apartment, you may bury your bottle in a large planter.

Ingredients:

+ A sturdy, clean, wide-mouthed bottle or jar—such as from mayonnaise, applesauce, or preserves—with a tight cover.

- Soil or sand from the area surrounding your home. In an apartment, you could use the soil from a potted plant.

- Something glittering and shiny, which you like or love; but this doesn't have to be valuable, nor do you need to sacrifice favorite jewelry. I have used a piece of beach glass, an odd discarded earring, a rhinestone—all objects I enjoy, but can easily part with.

- A rusty, bent nail. You can find rusty nails around construction sites; you may have to bend your find with a hammer. Careful—don't stick yourself! Now, whenever I see rusty bent nails, I am thrilled to take them home for future use.

- Assorted herbs—fresh if possible, but dried if necessary—sage, rosemary, thyme, parsley, and mint. Garlic is also traditional. Add herbs of your choice.

- A new penny or other coin (optional).

- A magical work candle.

To Proceed:

Light your candle, and ideally allow it to burn (safely) while you work. Say an appropriate Bottle Spell as you fill the bottle. Something such as:

With Goddess and God
(*Names of your Deities*)
Working for and through me
According to Free Will and For the Good of All

I now fill this bottle—

Earth (or sand) anchors this magic in the ground.

This rusty nail, bent, now repels anything and anyone
negative or life-denying.

This sparkling, shiny (name object) holds the light for
me, the light of my magic, and my Deities.

These herbs infuse the bottle with their living
properties—cleansing, purifying, consecrating,
and blessing.

This new penny (coin) manifests abundance in this, my
home.

This home is divinely protected and effectively safe.

Nothing and no one can enter or even touch it without
my permission

Only those people and beings through whom the Goddess and the God work

Can stay here

Can visit here

Can touch this place

Only Positive Magic and Positive Witchcraft live in
this place

In safety, protection, abundance, love, and joy

According to Free Will and For the Good of All

I now bury this bottle

It is invisible to all but me, and those I choose,

And its magic continues

And so mote it be.

By the time you have said your spell, the bottle should be buried, covered with leaves or something appropriate to make it truly invisible. Under the ground, it will continue to work until you choose to remove it. If you leave that area, it is best to dig up the bottle, adjust the contents appropriately, reconsecrate it, and bury it in your next place.

CHAPTER 12

Ritual

Almost everything in this book is a ritual, in the sense that we perform an act in microcosm with the express purpose of causing something similar to occur on a larger scale. Approaching this millennium time, people have been performing public rituals, which seem to have no purpose at all, other than to express a spiritual sentiment and unite a group of individuals who do the work. Some people do not expect any more than this from a ritual, in other words, no specific results, other than to draw attention to the subject. This can be a totally spiritual experience, but in my definition, this is not a ritual. This would be a *ceremony.* Many religious traditions are ceremonial in nature, such as lighting candles, saying grace, or reciting prayers of devotion (when not actually asking the Deity for something). The original meanings of some of these ceremonies may have been lost over the centuries. People may reenact something spiritual and feel good about it, but not really know why they do it, such as exchanging gifts at holiday time, or blowing out candles on a birthday cake. These ceremonies had profound meaning, usually in earlier Pagan Goddess–worshipping religions. But that is another story.

Many rituals are secular in appearance, yet they are true rituals in the old-fashioned sense. They do more than simply connect people; they have a goal. *We do this because we want that to happen.* Public demonstrations, protests, and marches are replete with homemade rituals. People dress up as whales or trees to save the environment, people lie down in coffins to demand AIDS research. These are original, powerful experiences, a response to a visceral need to do something, to make something happen—but not necessarily with an understanding of the process of ritual, what makes it work, and what makes it safe and ethical.

What is a Ritual?

Ritual is a bridge that takes you from where you are to where you want to be.

As Witches, we should be as careful and responsible when participating in anyone else's ritual, as we would be in creating our own. Rituals have power—that is the whole idea. The *participants* are as affected by a ritual as is the subject matter of the goal. I once got sick, literally came down with the flu, after participating in a ritual as a guest of a coven whose members didn't really know what they were doing. They called on some Deities with Whom they were not particularly aligned, Whose attributes they did not understand. They made conflicting statements and were shockingly inconsiderate of individual members' needs. This created a chaotic, seriously unpleasant atmosphere. Please be very careful with ritual. I have learned: If you don't like a ritual for any reason—don't do it!

Having said that, please enjoy your rituals fully. The joy of the ritual goes into the manifestation work, and gives you joyous results. That is why singing, dancing, chanting, and drumming work so well. They literally lift our spirits as we work. Rituals should always feel good.

Exceptions to this, of course, are rituals dealing with painful situations, such as funerals, memorials, some healings, and serious problems, including wars. But even these rituals are enlightening and comforting, at the very least. Always try to end every ritual on an uplifting note—not with denial, but with hope and affirmation for the Infinity of Solution.

Rituals should be agreed upon by all the participants. Some rituals are spontaneous, or contain spontaneous elements within them. Nonetheless, only those who sincerely wish to should participate.

Everybody who participates in a ritual should understand every tiny detail of it. Every word should be understood, and that goes for other languages, too. Remember the ritual at the end of the film, *Raiders of the Lost Ark?* When the ancient secret words were said over the ritual object, what happened? Nazi demons were unleashed! Or demons who liked Nazis; that part wasn't clear. But the point is, they were hideous, noisy, uncontrollable, and full of special effects—nothing you would want in your living room.

Every word in every song should be understood and agreed with, too. Or change the lyrics!

A ritual should contain a clearly stated purpose, a beginning, a middle, and an end—even if it's a very short ritual.

A ritual should be performed in sacred, blessed space, or space that has been somehow blessed and consecrated before-hand, however briefly. It can be a simple statement, such as, "I now call on the Goddess and the God to guide and protect us in this ritual and the situation it represents." Or you could turn out lights, burn sage, light incense, set up candles, call on all of your Deities and the Four Directions, invoke local nature spirits and ancestors, and carefully draw your Circle on the ground. It depends on the occasion, how much time you have, and what you want.

A ritual can be performed alone. For example, String Magic is a ritual. A ritual can also be performed with your coven, or with larger groups of people, as I have done on Halloween in comedy clubs—or with hundreds or even thousands of people, as I have done on radio and television. That's really like the old days! Public, group ritual is performed by the entire group; that is its Power. Today, rituals are even shared on the Internet. I look forward to rituals in outer space.

When leading or joining with non-Witches in a ritual, keep the work clear and simple; I usually say "Goddess and God" rather than say aloud the names of my Deities. In some groups I say, "The Universal Power" or "The One Power." There are many reasons for this: If people aren't one hundred percent aligned with your Deities, if people prefer to invoke what is sacred to them (which should always be encouraged), bringing in a Pagan pantheon could create too much confusion and be counter-productive—and unfair. Witchcraft is still a private religion. You can say the names to yourself, and for yourself, in silence.

Remember that *everything* going on during the ritual, vis-ibly and invisibly, goes into the work, and consequently into the results. This means words, thoughts, emotions, and feelings among the participants—including the way the participants feel toward each other. Sometimes during our coven work there could seem to be some tensions or worries in the room. Then one of us will add, "No harmful Power in such-and-such," with no judgment, of course. Also, if anyone disagrees with anything, it should be spoken, and openly discussed, at the appropriate moment. "I don't feel comfortable with this action, so I would prefer to do that instead." As a rule, rituals performed with coven members are more specific, and those performed with non-Witches are more general. You can see why the members of a coven should basically (*not superficially*) be in harmony, as a starting point.

If someone has originated the ritual, or is leading it, all participants should be very careful to see that Personal Power is respected in everyone. Never give Power away to a leader or even to the content of the ritual. Rituals found in books written by "experts" might be great, but I feel they can always use some personal customizing by you. If it's a well-composed ritual, this process can be a delicate balance. Again, if anything doesn't feel right, don't do it. The book may say, "Take off your clothes and drink wine," and you might not want to do this. Worse, the book might say, stop someone from doing something or make someone do something. But even if the book or the "expert" says something totally poetic and meaningful—if you simply read that, or repeat it in your ritual, then built into that process is some relinquishment of personal expression and usually Personal Power as well.

It is best to create your own rituals. *Your own!* That's where the Power is. Notice that I haven't included any instructions here. But I will tell you about some rituals we have done, and some that covens I know and respect have performed.

Tried and True Rituals

Blessing of a new baby: According to Free Will and For the Good of All—for health, protection, happiness, everything wonderful we could think of. Babies in covens don't automatically become Witches, by the way. They are honored guests until they eventually can make a choice. Needless to say, never pressure a child to join.

Handfasting: This is a Witchcraft marriage. Some Witches jump over a broom, as do many native peoples. Yes, there are legally licensed Witch and Pagan ministers now in the United States. And at any marriage, Wiccan or otherwise, it is so infinitely crucial to choose carefully what words are spoken over the wedding couple. Every idea will become a part of their marriage over the years. For example, one couple I know chose Edgar Allen Poe's "The Raven" to be read at their wedding. So many times was the word "Nevermore" repeated during the wedding ceremony, that the marriage ended shortly thereafter in divorce. Would they have divorced anyway? Nobody can prove anything like this, but just avoid negatives.

Blessing of a young girl on her first menstrual period: Every female member of my coven called on her Priestess Deity Alignment for that occasion. This was a women-only event.

Croning: A joyous celebration with drumming, singing, and dancing on the occasion of a woman or man turning fifty years old, and/or a woman entering menopause. This event celebrates wisdom, prolongs good health, and redefines older age, in general, as something truly wonderful.

Jumping on a broom and over a plant on Beltane: This aids all newly seeded crops, including all projects and new beginnings. This is also Fertility Magic for couples who want to have a child.

The Great Rite: This is an intensely personal ritual to be shared by a loving couple, two people who are dedicated both to each other and the work of Witchcraft. Usually, this is a handfasted couple. The traditional Great Rite in ancient times was apparently enacted by a heterosexual couple, although today, as we recreate our religion for modern times, a gay couple can manifest this sacred act as well. Essentially, this is the private experience of sexual love performed within a consecrated space or Circle. Some have used a pentagram drawn on the ground as their bed. The Circle is drawn and consecrated, each one dedicates himself/herself to the Goddess or the God, so the act represents the union of the two. A magical goal is set up beforehand. The idea is that the sexual energy that is raised by two loving Witches is the vehicle that manifests the goal. There is also room for chanting, dancing, drumming, Words of Power, and visualization within this ritual, if desired.

Purification of water from a local bay: We held cups of the water over our candles, and blessed them, then returned the waters to their source. Future lab tests showed success.

Burial or scattering of ashes and calling in a familiar or pet: I have done this several times, always According to Free Will and for the Good of All. They have most often returned to me.

Any event in life can be enriched with an appropriate ritual: The blessing of a new home or business, the planting of a garden, the dedication of an area where you will be staying or working. On request, I once cleansed and blessed a hockey stadium.

Ritual enriches life.

Personal Ritual: The Four Directions in the Morning

Many Witches call upon The Four Directions as part of a ritual, as part of opening the Circle, as part of a coven meeting. This specific use of the Four Directions is meant as a private combination ritual and meditation. It is a practice that helps with grounding, with connecting to nature—no matter where you are—with remembering personal Power, and it is also a wonderfully optimistic way to start the day.

I learned this practice from Selena Fox, the founder and director of Circle Sanctuary, and a highly respected Wiccan Priestess, among her many credentials. As she explained to me, and I now pass on to you, your own personal focus on each of the Directions is really up to you and your needs. The only part of this work that remains constant is facing North, East, South, and West—in that order. This may be the first time, you will need a compass!

So I will share with you the way in which I do it, and then you can add your own adjustments. I have found it best to work outdoors, but some mornings that is impossible, so standing near a window is fine. Privacy is important, unless of course you work with another Witch.

I face North, and hold out my arms in that direction, in a welcoming gesture, and say:

Spirits of the North, please bless me for perfect health
(*now I draw my arms inward, touching my head, heart, etc.*)
In body, mind, and spirit.
Even though with Goddess and God working for me and through me
I already manifest perfect health, Spirits of the North, please help
Thank you and So Mote It Be.

Then I turn to the East and repeat the gesture of holding out my arms:

Spirits of the East, please bless me for perfect wealth, financial security, and abundance of all kinds.
(*now, drawing my arms inward, touching my heart*)
Even through with Goddess and God working for me and through me
I already manifest perfect wealth, financial security, and abundance of all kinds Spirits of the East, please help
Thank you and So Mote It Be.

Next, I turn to face the South, with same gesture:

Spirits of the South, please bless me for manifest magical power of the Priestess, Witch, and Queen of My Realm and perfect wisdom
(*hands to heart*)

Even though with Goddess and God
Working for me and through me
I already manifest the magical power of the Priestess,
    Witch and Queen of my Realm and perfect wisdom
Spirits of the South, please help
Thank you and So Mote It Be.

Last, I turn to face the West, with the same welcoming
    gesture:

Spirits of the West, please bless me for perfect love,
    inside and outside
(*hands to heart*)
Even though with Goddess and God working for me
    and through me
I hereby manifest perfect love, inside and outside,
Spirits of the West, please help
Thank you and So Mote It Be.

Finally, I face North again and repeat four times:

From my true self to my true self . . .

then I repeat four times:
Now and forever . . .

And then:
Thank you and So Mote it Be. (once)

Note: I chose East for abundance, because in several
(Eastern) traditions, including Feng Shui, the East is the direction representing wealth.

Also, "love inside and outside" means love of self and then
love of—and from—others![1]

part two

Advanced Work

CHAPTER 13

Aspects of Self

According to the Aspect Theory, each of us has myriad lifetimes and personalities. However, contrary to the more popular beliefs about reincarnation, these lifetimes are not necessarily sequential—because time itself is not sequential. By sequential, I mean past moving to present moving to future. Human perception in our culture may experience time as sequential, and we may therefore assume that reincarnation is linear, but this is only perception. In the Aspect Theory and now in quantum physics as well—all time is considered to be actually simultaneous. In other words, although most people believe that time includes past, present, and future, all time is really made up of one vast present.

Among those of us who believe in reincarnation, the most popular belief is that some of our lifetimes have been lived in the past, one is going on right now, and the rest will all be lived in the future. But the Aspect Theory holds that actually *all* of our lifetimes are going on right now, although the only one that seems to be existing in the present is the one upon which we are focusing right now. Further, to reinforce this popular belief (that we each have only one present lifetime) most people have made *agreements* with most if not all of the others in their lives, and even with the rest of our society. These are unspoken and almost forgotten karmic agreements, to this effect: that everyone involved will focus together on this one lifetime, this one world, this one moment in history, as "now"—and that everything else will be considered "past" or "future."

Of course, with everyone around us focusing in the same way on one agreed-upon reality, this shared version of reality seems pretty compelling. In fact, any experience outside of this reality—any experience that somehow doesn't fit within our society's definitions of past, present, and future—is considered to be a dream or a fantasy. Occasionally, someone may happen to believe that such apparent dreams or fantasies seem valid—as real as, or even more real than, this one agreed-upon lifetime. This severely confused state can cause mental illness, including some forms of schizophrenia. I am not an expert on mental illness, but I know there are several types of schizophrenia. This is just one.

So determined is this culture to compartmentalize time as past, present, and future, that most people today feel it's inconceivable that time could possibly exist—or that life could ever be lived—any other way. But some people do believe that we can live outside of the past-present-future sequence. Proponents of the so-called New Physics have been brave enough to openly explore other dimensions and alternate universes. And for centuries, some occult and metaphysical studies have referred to *probable futures* and *alternate lives*.[1]

Personal Magic

I call this area "sideways in time." And in this area, we can now explore the phenomenon of *alternate lives*, which may also be defined as *co-existing lives*. These are variations on the one current lifetime we are living (focusing on) right now. Consider, for example, that we each have several alternate lives. All of these lives *co-exist* with the one present lifetime upon which each of us is focusing right now. What are these alternate lives like? Well, each of us has actually stepped "sideways" in time— however briefly—to experience them. We may have done this in dreams, particularly those compelling dreams, which seem so *real* to us. These are the kinds of dreams that seem to stay with us through most of the following day, or even longer. These are the dreams that catch our attention, and cause us to marvel at how surprisingly real such a dream has felt: Real, but somehow different from the agreed-upon present life. In dreams, alternate lives are exactly like our current lives. Well not exactly, because they always seem to contain a few variations that ultimately seem jarring or confusing. The surroundings may be the same as our daily surroundings, the time frame similar ("the present"), and most of our circumstances will match those of the lives we are consciously living now, except for a few significant changes. Perhaps certain family members or friends, who have passed on in this life, will be very much alive in the alternate life. Often we ourselves may seem a little bit different. We might have different names, be different ages than we are now, or even be a different gender.

When experiencing an alternate life in this type of dream, we may go along with it for a while. Then, in effect, we remember all of our other agreements—agreements we have had with many other people in this life—about what "reality" is, what our town really looks like, who is currently alive and who is dead, who is male and who is female, and everything else. We remember these agreements, and we miss our current lifetime, leave the dream reality, and return to our mutually-focused-upon present life.

This, of course, is only one explanation for dreams, and I do not mean to negate the numerous other meaningful explanations offered by psychological and metaphysical study.

But those people whose alternate lives may seem as real to them—or even more real—than this one particular lifetime, may also be labeled schizophrenic. Some of them may even be considered "multiple personalities." Of course I am not saying that all mental illness or even all cases of schizophrenia, or multiple personalities, can neatly be explained as misunderstanding a proper occult view of the Universe. Anyone who really cannot tell the difference between this lifetime and any other—past, present, future, or sideways in time:

1. Is not perceiving time as simultaneous in the positive sense, but instead in a confused way.
2. Is not in control of his/her perceptions, which seem to take over the rest of daily life.

However, it is possible to work with an informed understanding of alternate lives—and other lifetimes as well—in a way that greatly enriches the experience of this one current lifetime. This information is coming up shortly, but let us continue with background first.

To the extent that these things can be described in simple terms, we may say that *each of our many lifetimes—including* the apparent past, the mutually focused-upon present, and the probable future ones as well—*each of these has myriad alternate coexisting lives as variations on each lifetime.* These alternate lives may be seen as running parallel to each lifetime. If they are perceived, they do not seem to exist as past or future, but some sort of alternate present.

This adds up to plenty of lifetimes. And when you consider that they are all going on in the present, this certainly provides a lot of activity in the present. No wonder we need to focus on just one! To focus on more than one at a time, or even to believe that the potential for the others' existence is valid, could be just too disorienting. I do not mean to suggest that we attempt to enter into the other lifetimes. This is what happens "accidentally," for brief time periods, without clear planning, such as in dreams as previously mentioned. This is also what happens when a person crosses over into another life and back again several times, and then is not sure which life he/she is in, or who he/she really is—the resident of this life or the resident of that one. Mental hospitals are full of people who are apparently experiencing this. Another more serious problem can be the temptation to enter into another lifetime and then remaining there, to live there "fulltime" by perceiving that lifetime exclusively. From the vantage point of those people left behind in this current lifetime, that appears to be death. And it is, in this regard: the person who does this leaves this plane entirely (although the body stays here). Therefore, it is dangerous to enter into other lifetimes, and it is not necessary to do so, either. There is another, much better way to experience the benefits that the understanding and knowledge of these other lifetimes can offer us.

How the Aspect Theory Works

According to the Aspect Theory, we believe that *part of ourselves is actually already living fully in—and focusing thoroughly on—every single one of our other lifetimes.* The theory is based on the fact that the soul is infinite; each one of us has a huge, ageless, wise, and profound soul. The soul is the sum total of all of its parts. Many parts exist, each living out a different lifetime. Each one of the parts is a full personality unto itself, and each is called an *aspect of the self.* So, according to this theory, in each and every one of your lifetimes, there now exists a specific *aspect* of yourself. Each aspect is a distinct personality, as distinct as your personality in this current lifetime. Put all your *aspects* together and they add up to your soul.[2]

Each aspect of the self has had different experiences and has developed different areas of expertise. Some are talented, some are wise; some are highly evolved because they live in what we call the future. Many aspects of ourselves have a great deal to teach us, if we could only contact them. And we can, because all of our lifetimes are taking place right now, so all of our aspects are very much alive right now. In working with aspects, this is exactly what we do. We communicate with various aspects of ourselves who live (have lived, will live, simultaneously now live) in our other lifetimes. We communicate with these aspects in a careful and controlled way, never losing our primary focus on our current personality in our current, agreed-upon lifetime. We are watchful not to confuse the current personality (aspect) self with any other aspect. We do not want to fuse aspects, or experience two or more lifetimes simultaneously. We want,

Personal Magic

instead, to *communicate* from the vantage point of this one personality in this one current lifetime—with aspects of our selves who live in other lifetimes. We do this to learn, to benefit from what is actually our own infinite wisdom, and to enrich our lives. Which lives get enriched, you may ask? This, our primary-focus, current lifetime? Yes, of course, and this is a most immediately rewarding, comforting, and generally fabulous technique for problem solving. But we also get so much more. Once we begin working with aspects of the self, we realize that *enriching one lifetime automatically enriches all our other lifetimes.*

It can be difficult to measure or even describe the effects of such work. We can say it "enriches the soul" or even "speeds up the evolution of the soul." But then we realize that the soul in all time is already so highly evolved, that it is already perfect. We also realize that the idea of speeding up the evolutionary process of the soul is actually an illusion, because the future co-exists with the present simultaneously (not to mention with the past as well), so there is no need to "speed up" anything! Meditate or think about this information so far, and you can see that the very contemplation of such ideas is incredibly liberating, and provides us with glimpses of infinite possibilities for growth, for experience, and for nourishment. This is truly Selene's domain, where anything is possible. The English language, as we know it in this one lifetime, may be limited in describing these concepts. But experiencing this work—or even considering the possibility of such experience—transcends any need for description.

How to Work with
Aspects of the Self

As stated earlier, this work is not for everyone, and you may wish to meditate upon the information already given and not decide to go any further, not to bring it into practice, which is fine.

If you feel unsure about working with aspects, you may consult an oracle, such as *The I Ching*, tarot cards, or pendulum to help decide.

If you feel ready to work with aspects, I have found the best way to do this is with a partner, one who feels completely ready also, preferably who is a Witch, and who has studied the previous background material. Someone from your coven might be appropriate. The motives of you both should be to achieve personal growth and understanding. You should be comfortable working with each other, and all work must be kept confidential and private. This means neither one of you should even consider telling anyone else about what transpires in this work, unless it is by mutual consent. Mutual trust, respect, and consideration are also essential. If you don't feel completely comfortable about working with a specific aspect partner (or vice versa), then wait until the right partner is revealed. If no partner is revealed this time, then you may send out a Words of Power Call for the appropriate partner.

Here are the guidelines according to which my aspect partner and I work. If you wish to make any variations on the details of these arrangements, just be sure that your changes are for the good of all, according to free will, and in keeping with the most positive essence of aspect work.

We have found it best to work on a regular basis. When we began this work, for several years we set aside two hours every week, the same evening every week, and the same time—to the best of our ability. However, you may not feel it necessary to work as frequently as we did in compiling our original research. You may prefer to work only when a feeling of need arises (which is what we do now). But no matter what the timing, two hours for a session is recommended, one hour for each of you.

Plan that each of the hours will be uninterrupted. Try to take a break only after the first hour's work is completed. The reason for this is that concentration with aspects can be very intense, and difficult to maintain in the face of interruptions or distractions.

Before you start, it's a good idea to select an area of your life that you wish to work on. This will be true for each of you. This then, is the subject you will discuss with your aspect. You may have several items on your agenda. Any subject matter is absolutely fine, but of course it's best to choose situations for which there seems to be no explanation or solution having to do with this lifetime. Have a pad and pen handy, a recording device, or computer (or even a typewriter, but only if it is silent). During your session, your partner will record your work, and during your partner's session, you will record. Each of you should keep your own notes for further study. Do not rely on memory! Due to its essentially dream-like or trance-like quality, aspect work can be difficult to remember later. If you're taking notes, try to make them as accurate as possible.

Work in a semi-darkened room, in absolute quiet and privacy. There should be a space to lie down or lean back in total comfort, which you will take turns doing. You may find you

want a blanket or other cover. No one other than your partner should be present. Phones should be shut off or somehow
answered without you hearing the ring. No background music,
no television, no whistling tea kettles! Your work tools can be
present—your familiar, crystals, and any magical aids. You may
have one Work or Goddess candle lit during the work. If you are
concerned for any reason about burning a flame for such a long
time period, then blow it out after the Opening Blessing:

Words of Power for Aspect Work
(*State Alignments, then add:*)
We hereby call on You, our Deities,
To work for us and through us
And through all of our Aspects
We call on the most perfect Aspects
For perfect communication
In all time and all space
For the Good of All
And According to Free Will
We are all hereby divinely protected
And divinely guided
As this work answers all our mutual and individual
     needs,
We thank you.
And so mote it be!

Make a note of the time when the first person begins. No
matter how frequently or infrequently you work, the other person should begin first the next time, and you should continue
to take turns. This is for fairness and equal opportunities to

benefit from this aspect work. Of course, make exceptions for emergencies.

If you are first this time, your partner makes a note of the time, and more or less watches the clock during your hour. Your partner takes notes, or records the session. You lean back, close your eyes, and relax totally. Then say:

> I am now calling on an aspect of myself, the most perfect, positive and appropriate one, in perfect communication, to help me with this matter (*state subject of concern*).

Stay relaxed, eyes closed. Your partner should be quiet. At this point, the appropriate Aspect will probably appear to you. Most likely, this will first take place with an image.

You may visualize a person. Try to have no preconceptions, and try not to discard whatever image appears as mere imagination. You may not get a clear image every time, but you will definitely get a strong sense of presence. The Aspect may or may not look like you, but it is a part of you nonetheless. Listen to find out whether the Aspect speaks. This occurs in a silent yet distinct inner voice. Sometimes, there is no image—just the voice. When it does speak, then report aloud to your partner what the Aspect is saying.

You may ask the Aspect questions. If so, say your question aloud, listen for the inner voice of the answer, and then report the answer to your partner for the record. After a while, the process will become comfortable and easy for you. You may want your partner to help by asking the Aspect some questions, or to encourage you to describe the Aspect and its surroundings. However, your partner should mostly remain quiet.

You may want to know what life the Aspect comes from, and what its circumstances are in that life. But mainly the Aspect is there to give you advice, and you should feel free to ask anything at all. This is one reason that the choice of partners is so crucial; you should feel completely comfortable discussing *anything* with your Aspect in front of your partner.

If your Aspect partner does help with the questioning process, this should be only at your request, and with a Witch's true discretion. At all times, the focus of the work should remain on you during your hour, so your partner does not ask for advice at this time. You and your Aspect should do most of the talking. The same is true for your partner's hour.

It is best to use one-point concentration during this work, focusing solely on your Aspect and your communication. Everything else, such as keeping notes, should be left up to your partner. Consequently, this process may feel like a trance or deep meditation, and you should allow yourself to exit from it gradually. You will probably sense when your hour is up. Of course, you don't have to be rigid about this; some sessions might take longer, some less time. Usually your Aspect will tell you when it's appropriate to close. Your partner may remind you *gently*.

When you feel you have received enough clear information from your Aspect, which usually occurs toward the end of your session, work Words of Power to the effect that you release all difficulties surrounding the problem(s) and transform Negatives into Positives, replacing each difficulty with the appropriate solution.

Something such as this:

Closing Aspect Blessing
With the One Power which is Goddess and God
Working for me and through me
I hereby give thanks for this aspect work
And affirm that I have learned all that I need to know
    at this time.
I release all cause, effects, manifestation, forms, and
    essences of (*name situation or problem*)
And I now replace it all with (name goals)
I completely turn this all to good
According to free will
And for the good of all
And so mote it be.
(*Always thank your Aspects.*)

Your Aspect will probably recede from your focus as the work ends, and at this point you may feel yourself drifting or floating—or a similar sensation. Keep your eyes closed. Allow your reentry to be gradual. To aid this transition, one of my Aspects gave me this handy image of a tunnel: Picture a long and beautiful tunnel (as through a mountainside in the country), and let one entrance to the tunnel be at the far end, which is the place where you have met with your aspect. The near end of the tunnel is the room in which you and your partner are sitting. Allow yourself to gradually glide through the tunnel, as if on ultra-smooth railroad tracks, until you get to the end, which is near your room. Then open your eyes.

At this point, you and your partner may wish to take a short intermission, and then resume the work. This time, you will be the one with the clock, the notes, or the recording device, and your partner will be the one reclining, with eyes closed, to communicate with his/her aspect. This time, all focus will be on your partner, and you will speak only to help, and only if clearly requested to do so. The process will be the same for your partner as for you, with Words of Power at the appropriate point. After the (approximate) hour is past, you may remind your partner of the time, with the utmost gentleness. Allow your partner to take all the time needed for re-entry. Make a note of who worked first so that the next time the sequence may be reversed.

After you really get used to this work, you may find, as my Aspect partner and I did, that it's possible to conduct your sessions effectively over the telephone. We still prefer to work in person, but we'd much rather work on the phone than not work at all.

Aspect work tends to be more reliable working with a partner than alone. If an Aspect appears spontaneously when you are alone, that is fine, but I still find it a rare occurrence. Instead, we have had occasions when an Aspect of mine briefly "visited" my partner in a moment of her (my partner's) need, and conversely her Aspect has been available to me when I needed her. However, these Aspects are most often from this current lifetime—so this is more like a mental visit from a friend than the more intense Aspect work itself.

Some Warnings About Aspect Work

Although this process may resemble some forms of trance mediumship, channeling, psychotherapy, or even psychic reading, Aspect work is not intended to be used toward any of these ends. It is not to be performed in a hierarchical setting, with one person leading and the other following or being "helped." Both partners are equals, and are to help themselves equally. Actually, each one is to be helped by his/her own aspect, and the direction this takes is essentially to be left up to the aspect(s). No exchange of money should ever take place. Aspect work is only to be done with Words of Power used to protect and direct the work and its participants, and only when both partners fully understand the Aspect Theory upon which it is based. And of course, Aspect work should only be done if both partners want to do it in the first place.

Of course you don't have to adhere rigidly to every detail of the Aspect Theory exactly as I explained it; eventually you will probably want to add changes of your own. But I consider it necessary to know the reasons for embarking on this work, and the structure of thought upon which it is based—as a starting point. And never, *never* insist that another person's Aspect has visited you unless the other person concurs that this has indeed happened. All sorts of hallucinations and manipulation can result from a misuse of Aspect work.

CHAPTER 14

Working Magic in the Castle

I have heard that some traditional English covens visualize a castle and then mentally go inside that castle to do their magical work. My coven and I have developed this technique in our own way, and I hope you will feel free to make any adjustments you wish. We now prefer to do all our work in the castle—whether individually, in a group, or in pairs, as when we call upon each other for help over the phone.

First, consecrate your work according to your Deity Alignments, including the goals of *protection* and *safety*. Then, close your eyes and visualize a beautiful castle. It doesn't have to match anybody else's vision of a traditional European castle. This is *your* castle. It can be an old, new, or renovated castle; it can be made of crystal, glass, bricks, wood, stone, or some outer space material. It doesn't matter. It is your castle, so allow yourself to visualize it freely.

You can visualize yourself approaching it on foot, on horseback, in a car, in a plane, however you wish. Or you can picture yourself immediately inside it, although I usually first perceive and experience my approach. The point is to ultimately work magic inside the castle. Picture yourself inside it, with the interior all around you. Try to feel it, touch it, and smell it. Walk through the rooms. Go up or down the stairs (or the elevators). The people or creatures you see in there are your special helpers and loved ones. My castle has the following rooms: A Great Hall in which to hold meetings and do work, a Courtyard in which to proclaim Words of Power to the realm, a Healing Room with a magical Healing Fountain in which to place oneself or loved ones (only with permission) to perform healings, a Ritual Room in which to light candles and perform rituals to echo the work we do in this realm, and a Treasury in which to work money, abundance, and Wealth Magic. Mine also has parapets from which I can survey the landscape, and a moat. Feel free to create any details you like. Just understand that the walls of the castle are lined with the concept *According to Free Will and for the Good of All*" so that all the magic that is worked in the castle follows this tenet. In my castle, I have advisors, and I mentally consult with them. In your castle, you can also have one or more wise women, men, or other beings with whom to discuss any subject and work magic.

Life in the Castle

Sometimes I mentally go into my castle and just look around, to see what it looks like that day, and to observe what the weather is outside the windows—which doesn't always correspond to the weather in everyday reality, by the way. Then I observe the activity within the castle, and read it as an oracle, or a dream, interpreting it to see what meaning this holds for my life. You can also go into your castle to direct and create circumstances, as you want them to be. For example, if you are planning an event in your life, such as a party or a meeting, you can first hold that event in the castle, and *non-manipulatively* talk to the invisible beings who appear, telling them how you want this event to take place. These are castle beings, not people from the world of form. Then watch events unfold.

The whole coven can sit together and visualize the castle at the beginning of each meeting. There is really no limit to what you can do in the castle—except that it always has to be *according to free will and for the good of all.*

Where is the castle? It is Between The Worlds.

Healing in the Castle

When you do healing in the castle, with permission, you can "place" people or animals in the Healing Fountain. At first, just observe them, because you can actually tell what their condition is by how well they seem to respond to the healing waters. You may see that they actually want to get up and leave; then you know you shouldn't even be doing this work for them. They may appear to become revived and return to health as they sit there, and then you know they're going to get better. They may seem to decline or sink in the water, which can indicate that their need may not be to recover according to your wishes. In such a case, you may still bless them and, if appropriate, continue to do the healing work "according to (name)'s needs and for the Good of All." You probably should bless yourself as well, in order to deal with whatever the loved one's choice may be.

You can call helpers into any of the castle rooms to work with you, but they should be denizens of the castle, not actual people whom you know in this life—because that would be manipulative. However, if actual people whom you know in this life do seem to appear to you in the castle—then as with any oracle or any dream—listen, interpret, work with, and later tell them about it (if that's appropriate) in the World of Form. You may find that people who have moved on to spirit may also appear in the castle, and possibly communicate with you.

There is no limit to the Positive Magical work you can do in your castle.

CHAPTER 15

Advanced Manifestation

This section may be viewed as an amplification of the Words of Power work found in my book, *Positive Magic*, and also the Words of Power work described earlier in this Book of Shadows. Not everyone may feel ready to work in this way, and some Witches may choose categorically never to do so, which is fine. There is certainly no judgment on this. I consider this work to be "Advanced" because it took me longer to develop than the techniques that I have written about up until now. Also, this work is more readily understood after achieving a foundation in those earlier techniques. I certainly was not ready to work like this for a long time, so I understand that others may feel the same way.

Magic is Transformation

Inspired by Marshall MacLuhan who said, "The medium is the message," I realized *The Witch is the magic.* First of all, Marshall MacLuhan was referring to a different kind of medium than I happen to be, or that you might be! He meant a communication medium such as television or film. MacLuhan realized that television itself is the message, not what you see on it; and film itself is also the message, not what you see in it. This is true, because the forms of television or movies—the technical way in which the images are formed in each—influence the people who are watching in subtle, distinct ways. And, in effect, the way the images are formed dictates what the true message will be: on film, on television, and in other media as well. Each medium is different, and the effects of each one on its audience are different. And this has nothing to do with the *content* of what is being broadcast, of what has been filmed, or of what is being seen or heard. This message (that of the medium itself) is what really influences the audience.

Now, I have often defined magic as the work of transformation.[1] For the early alchemists, this work was apparently the act of transforming base metals into gold. I say "apparently," not because this couldn't be done, but because it actually was accomplished by certain alchemists. I mean that transforming base metals into gold *appeared to be* the ultimate goal of alchemy—to the uninitiated. To the master alchemists, the true transformation was the transformation of the alchemist himself, or herself, to a higher level of consciousness. And this personal transformation is the actual goal of alchemy.

The same applies to any true magician. Ceremonial Magicians know this; Wizards and Shamans of many cultures know this, too. Yes, it's true that magic can actually transform matter and energy from one state to another, or make things seem to appear or disappear. But far more important is the fact that *magic transforms the magician*. With each magical working the magician is transformed further, and grows to a higher state of personal evolution. For the Witch, the work of magic usually involves transforming that which exists in the Invisible World, into the World of Form. And with each act of transformation, the Witch is transformed also, into an ever more advanced state. This understanding should be part of every Witch's awareness, with every magical act one does.

The Witch Is the Magic

To continue with this analogy, if "the medium is the message"—in other words, if the vehicle through which the message comes is really the message itself—then, in alchemy, we could say that the vehicle (the alchemist) through whom the message comes is really the message itself (transformation). The transformation of the alchemist is, as the alchemist would be the first to tell you, the goal of the work. The alchemist embodies this goal. So this is the true message, not the *content* of alchemy as found in the history books (written by outsiders, rather than alchemists), claiming that the goal was changing base metal into gold.

So the alchemist is the transformation. So also, the Ceremonial Magician is the transformation, the Wizard is the transformation, and the Shaman is the transformation. And of course, the Witch is the transformation! Each one of these magical workers is the transformation. And furthermore, because magic and transformation are one and the same, then each of these magical workers is the magic. The Witch, with whom we are concerned, is the magic. You are the magic. I am the magic. We can assume this as a somewhat inventive extrapolation of

Marshall MacLuhan's extraordinary insight, and leave it at that. Or we can explore the truth of this statement deeply enough to "own" it; that is, to understand it on such a profound level that it becomes part of our psyches. We then can apply it to ourselves.

So let us explore "the medium is the message." Can that idea be extended to religion too? Can we then say, "The prayer is the religion?" I think we can. Prayer is the apparent medium for the message, but the structure of the religion itself is the message. That is, the structure of the religion is a model of the worldview, which the religion really advocates. Let's try it. Pick a prayer, a traditional Western prayer that we might have said in school (at a time when prayers were said in school, or in a school where prayers were said). Such a prayer might well have started "Heavenly Father . . ."

Now, before we go any further, what is the message of this prayer so far—looking not at the content, but at the *structure of the religion, which the prayer's content reveals?*

1. The Deity is viewed as a parent (therefore the person is considered a child in comparison).

2. The parent is male (therefore either men are more important here, or perhaps there aren't any women present).

3. The Deity is in heaven (so, presumably, the person praying is not).

This is all part of the message of this prayer, just at its barest beginning. And if the prayer is the medium through which the message of that religion comes, then all the points mentioned previously are actually part of the message of the religion. Now, the religion might have a whole list of traditional tenets, which are presented officially, in order to define that religion. But another way to define that religion would be to look carefully at the *wording* of its prayers, and to also look at the *structure of life* as revealed through its prayers. What you get then would also be the message of that religion, and might, in fact be the most accurate message of that religion.[2]

Now, back to magic. We can do the same thing. We can explore the structure of life within any tradition, as revealed through its magic. Because I am not an alchemist, not a Ceremonial Magician, nor a Wizard or Shaman of any other tradition, I will deal now with Witchcraft. *The Witch is the magic.* This is true on several levels. Let us look at them one-by-one.

Magic is Manifestation

If the general definition of magic is transformation, then the specific kind of transformation used primarily by the Witch is manifestation. Further, Witchcraft is a nature religion; we work closely with the forces of nature, as they manifest on our planet Earth (which is one of the reasons I call my work Earth Magic). Our rituals are performed on the Earth Plane, our work goes out into the Invisible Realm, but it is always "grounded," it always returns to Earth, manifesting here. Thus, for the Witch, we may categorically say: *Magic is manifestation.*

Methods of Manifestation

We Witches do not have exclusive rights to the work of manifestation on this planet. Other magical and spiritual traditions work with manifestation, also. So do some religions. And so do some people who do not "believe in" magic at all—or who do not wish to be associated with it—yet they openly work with manifestation.[3]

The work of manifestation, an understanding of it, even an awareness of its existence by any stretch of the imagination, could not be, at this time, considered important in our culture. Nonetheless, some versions of manifestation do appear in contemporary thought, as follows:

1. In traditional Western religion, the idea of manifestation appears in the concept of prayer. God is asked to manifest that for which the faithful pray.

2. In "Positive Thinking" and related popular philosophies, the fundamental belief is that a positive mental and emotional attitude will manifest the desired results by "attracting" to a person the positive situations and material goods one wants.

3. In the so-called "Science" Religions, the word "science" applies to a view of religion as a science—presumably to define religion as somehow more realistic and modern, rather than "merely" spiritual. These religions include Christian Science, Religious Science, and a number of offshoots, including Jewish Science. In these practices, a person defines one's self as an embodiment of Deity, usually defined as God, Christ, or simply "Mind." Or the person might declare that Deity is within one's self. Instead of prayer, the terms "treatment" and "affirmation" are used. These techniques are employed for many positive

Personal Magic

manifestations, such as healing, and are also strongly associated with the manifestation of money and material goods.

4. In popular New Age and metaphysical studies: These include books, home study courses, tapes, classes, etc. Some are good, some are terrible (by Positive Witchcraft standards); yet all undeniably draw upon actual manifestation techniques, most often visualization. The instructions that I dub terrible, teach manipulation and the "influencing" of others as a means of getting what one needs and wants. The better ones are diluted or distorted versions of older occult traditions that are used to manifest the fulfillment of personal needs, mostly on a material level.

Many of the previously mentioned beliefs, techniques, practices, and studies are based upon what most of these groups call "The Law of Attraction" (or some variation on this term). Essentially, this cosmic legislation states that *like attracts like;* that one can *draw* to oneself whatever one needs or wants, if one uses this law "creatively." The belief is that everything exists (in potential, at least) somewhere in the Universe, and all one needs to do is name and/or visualize the thing one needs or wants, and affirm that one can and will get it. The goal might be a material object, or it might be an intangible state, such as health or love.

The techniques for making this happen are as varied as the schools of thought that teach this work, just a few of which are mentioned above. With prayer, an *unquestioning faith* in Deity is usually invoked, joined with one's own firm belief that one deserves such bounty. With the other, less overtly "religious" practices, the faith is in the Law of Attraction itself, and in one's ability to work with it—which actually might also have something to do with faith in the way that one has been taught to use said Law. *Concentration* is usually important: Visualizing the desired object (if tangible), in detail, is recommended; perhaps even getting physically close to a source of it. For example, I once attended a sermon by a reverend in such a semi-religious group. Jeweled rings flashing, he told the congregation that the way he attracted money into his life was to walk around the financial district and to hang around banks! And he recommended that we all do the same.

For those who choose to conceptualize Deity as within oneself, and for those who conceptualize Deity as Divine or Universal Mind, the work still may be done in a church-like setting with a minister in charge. Private counselors or "practitioners" may be engaged for a fee, and tithing (giving a percentage of one's income) to the religious institution may be encouraged or even required, especially if the manifestation work for money has been successful.

In some New Age and metaphysical branches of manifestation technique, visualization is categorically recommended—specifically visualization of oneself within the desired setting or holding the desired object. And again, faith in the Law of Attraction is usually as unquestioned as in the law of gravity.

All of these techniques of manifestation can, and most often do, work fairly effectively when belief is strong. The main problem seems to be that most of these practices do not make clear the importance of the concept of *form and essence* in choosing goals to manifest. Consequently, the people who work in these ways are often able to manifest material goods (forms) without solving their deeper feelings of dissatisfaction (essence). Because their innate perception of how much material goods they are actually able to attain remains untouched, they often are able to manifest their material goals only up to a point.

I now have a name for these forms of manifestation, which work in a "non-magical" context. I call this Affinity Manifestation.

It is possible that some forms of Witchcraft may be practiced in ways that are similar to the methods just mentioned, and therefore may be considered Affinity Manifestation. I do not believe this could have been said more than a thousand years ago (give or take a few hundred years), when Witchcraft was a younger religion and its belief system was more intact. But many Witches today are converts from Judeo-Christian traditions and they may still carry with them the messages of those religions, at least for a while. However, the attributes of Wiccan Deities are vastly different from those of the patriarchal Deity. Specifically, the Goddess is so categorically beneficent and non-judgmental that Her very presence in the minds and beliefs of Witches causes a subtle change in their practice of manifestation. And this change eventually makes a vital difference between the way a Positive Witch works and the way another person might work, although their approaches may seem quite similar to the unschooled observer. In time, a Witch's work might organically grow beyond Affinity Manifestation. Let's see if we can aid the process.

Two Levels of Manifestation

1. Affinity Manifestation

2. Creation Manifestation

I am going to describe the two in detail, so you can tell in which category you have been working, and so you may learn how to change your category, should you wish. First, I have to say that a clear delineation into two distinct categories is not entirely possible in Witchcraft, because there are many overlapping areas. Some of us may manifest one way some of the time, and another way the rest of the time, depending on the context in which we do our work. Even when following the Words of Power techniques, which I teach, a person could still move from one type of manifestation work to the other.

And actually, I think that basically it doesn't matter. I have always thought that magic in itself is such a wonderful gift, and that the Witch's special kind of magic—manifestation—is so remarkable, that just to know about it in the first place is fabulous enough. And to be able to practice it at all—in this culture, on this planet, and at this time—is transcendent.

And yet, I often found myself wondering: How can I transform myself, as Priestess and Witch, into an even higher state of development? How can I make my work even more consistently effective, and how can I teach others to do this, too?

I worked Words of Power for this goal. In time, research and more practice revealed that a subtle change in atmosphere was beginning to take place. Soon it became possible to recognize certain drawbacks in performing Words of Power—specifically for manifestation work—when this new atmosphere did not seem to be present. I do not mean to imply that Words of Power ever did not work. They always work. But a certain effectiveness and clarity, and a feeling of almost incredible harmony, could be very obviously felt as part of the work, to varying degrees—or sometimes could seem to be missing. Maybe some of you know what I am talking about; it seems really elusive to describe. And I'm sure it is different for different people. At times, I could almost recognize a sort of "buzzing" in the air around me that engendered a unique state of peace, of stillness and concentration. I can describe it as an atmosphere, a "mindset," and as a feeling. Often, this seemed to have something to do with the presence of other Positive Witches working together. I felt it when working with my coven, but not consistently. I felt it intensely when I attended the First International Goddess Conference in 1982, surrounded by approximately 1,000 Witches and Goddess-worshippers working in group ritual under the open sky, truly sacred ground. The feeling also stayed with me after I came home. It could be evoked with a memory of certain work at the Conference. And later, the feeling also emerged during my first research in aspect work. In fact, the continued aspect work seemed to develop it more fully. So, with this new development, I noticed that my process of the work of Words of Power seemed to have changed for the better.

Eventually I realized that whenever this feeling had been present during Words of Power work, the manifestations seemed to come much more swiftly than before. Also, the quality of the manifestations seemed subtly altered. Now (this feels almost impossible to describe, but please bear with me), I could say that the manifestations began to take on a more "delightful" quality, but I do not mean to denigrate, in any way, the quality of manifestation work done before, which was always wonderful. I can only say that both the process, and the results of my work (the manifestations), seemed to have somehow changed for the better.

And further, the overall process of transformation of the Witch—in this case, me—felt different, also.

Now I know what to call this phenomenon. It is the work of *Creation Manifestation*. More accurately, this is what Creation Manifestation *feels like*. It is a new level, representing new growth and development. I suppose that one could start out at this level, and learn how to work Words of Power in this way in the first place. But I suspect that at this time, in this particular culture, this might be difficult.[4]

I think that at this moment in linear time, we probably need to progress from Affinity Manifestation to Creation Manifestation. Also, as noted earlier, it may be true that for a Witch, both kinds of manifestation will probably be operative in an overlapping way, at least for a while. This will be the process until the Witch is ready to recognize and maintain the level of Creation Manifestation exclusively—*if desired*.

For me, the recognition of this level meant a consistent and dramatic change. However, a very important point to make is that I had really been working in this way, from time to time—all along. But I was not always aware that I was doing this, and part of the impact of working with Creation Manifestation is the conscious awareness of using it. Even though we can delineate two levels of manifestation work, most of us have experienced many mixtures of working on both levels. We really cannot label the way we work each time. That is not the point. The point is to learn everything we can about Creation Manifestation, so that if we choose to do so, we can work at this level all the time. And we also need to know all we can about Affinity Manifestation, so that we may consciously choose to use it when we wish. Then if we want to move beyond it, the choice will be clear.

Personal Magic

Affinity Manifestation

Remember the Law of Attraction? Any form of manifestation work, which is based on this Law, is Affinity Manifestation. But many other techniques, which might not specifically mention the Law of Attraction, still fall into this category. That is, if they are based upon a belief that manifestation is brought about by a process of consciously *drawing* to you that which you need. Now, this in itself is a revolutionary idea to many people in our culture, and it has provided a positive force for good, which is not to be minimized. But as I see it, Affinity Manifestation has one major drawback: If you believe, in essence, that somewhere out in the Universe exists that which you need or want, and you must now do specific work to draw it to you—then you might possibly lapse into sensing a feeling of *distance* between your current situation and that which you want to achieve. You might experience intense need or lack. You might have an awareness that now, as you are doing this work, you do not yet have this "thing," or this goal, or whatever the end result you want might be. You might feel, "It's not here yet. It's still *out there.*" And attached to this feeling might be, "Gee, I feel terrible that it's not here yet!" Or even, "Maybe it will never manifest."

Now, if the medium is indeed the message, then this perception of lack that one might feel *while doing the work,* might go right into the work, and this can manifest, too—as delay. Another way of saying this is that focusing on the current state of not-having can perpetuate that very state. Even if you don't actually say, "I feel a sense of distance from my goal," the pain of feeling that distance (or even a mild discomfort) might well go into the work. This can be very difficult to avoid. I have experienced it many times. Before I learned about Creation Manifestation, the antidote I always used was to work Words of Power to release the pain, the doubt, the perception of distance, or whatever that discomfort felt like. Then I would replace that with confidence, Deity Alignments, The Infinity of Solution, and any other positive ideas that seemed appropriate. This technique is completely effective, and still recommended. However, the problem here could be that one *might not* notice certain moods of doubt or lack. These feelings can be insidiously subtle and difficult to watch out for, because of their elusive nature and the state of malaise they can induce. In other words, the feeling of lack could *sneak into* the Words of Power, unnoticed, and one might not recognize the necessity to include the antidote work. Too often, unusual delays in manifestation can be traced to this very cause.

Consequently, the entire progress of self-transformation might also be delayed. You may well ask, *How can such timing be measured?* Also, what's an appropriate pace for self-transformation in a Witch, anyway? I would say, if one feels a true sense of dissatisfaction in one's own personal growth, this might be evidence of delay. The ideal pace, in my opinion, *feels right.* This is purely a matter of perception, so only you will know. No one can ever possibly tell you what your rate of development "should" be—especially in magic or in self-transformation.

If you have diagnosed your work up until now as Affinity Manifestation, and wish to learn Creation Manifestation, what is required first is a conceptual shift. Creation Manifestation begins with a different mindset than Affinity Manifestation. The "buzzing," the mood, the atmosphere and feeling—

everything I tried to describe earlier—is definitely present. These words may describe how a Witch *feels* when learning the new level of work. But in my opinion, this is not the most effective starting place. The true starting place is with an idea.

Creation Manifestation

This is an expression of a truly holistic view of the Universe. At this level of work, the Oneness of all of Creation is affirmed. There is no separation. We are all linked; all is connected. Thus there is no separation between you and that which you wish to work for. You are Goddess, you are God: You *create.* You do not draw your goal to you because it is not separate from you. You manifest yourself *as that goal;* you create it.

Creation is Perception

This is how it works: First of all, there is no massive ego misunderstanding (*"Hey, look at me, I'm a powerful Deity Incarnate!"*) because every living being is capable of working at this level, certainly in potential. In fact, every being *does* work at this level, but not necessarily with the awareness that this is what we are all doing. Remember the Aspect Theory? Remember that the basis of that theory is essentially this: *We create our current lifetimes by means of perceiving them.* So we may all acknowledge that we create our current *realities* by perception also. And this is an ongoing process.

We may now direct our perception in three ways:

1. We acknowledge that the process of directed perception is a means to creation.

2. We consciously choose to direct our perception in a certain way.

3. The way we do this is to identify ourselves as the very goal for which we are working.

Let's look at step 3 further. *We become the goal we are working for.* We acknowledge that we *already are* the goal we are working for. We focus on being that goal. We are it. Now, does this mean that we are no longer ourselves, that we have somehow become the goal instead? Not at all. We are ourselves *plus* the goal. Here is another way to look at this concept.

Zen and the Art of Tennis

A new technique that some tennis players use to vastly improve their game, is a sporty version of Zen meditation. The idea is that instead of focusing on their intense desire to hit the ball, they focus instead on the ball itself. They focus, in fact, on "being" the ball. In their mind's eye, they *become* the ball. Thus, they free themselves from trying to hit the ball, trying so hard that they actually can no longer hit it (this, it seems, is a common tennis problem). And once they stop trying, *that's* when they hit the ball! The idea is that when one tries too hard, one might not be able to accomplish something which one is perfectly capable of doing. Trying is what gets in the way. Trying is a "pre-effort;" not the effort itself. Instead of trying, the process of *being* the goal (in this case, the tennis ball) releases the self from getting bogged down in trying too hard, and allows the self to do what it has been capable of doing all along. In tennis, that is hitting the ball—and in our case, it is achieving any goal in the most effective and transforming way.

Let's approach it from yet a slightly different angle. We are creating what we want, rather than drawing it to us. So we have decided to become that "thing" we want, that goal, whatever it is—in our minds. First, it is helpful to visualize it. Artists all know how to do this. As the saying goes, any work of art, before it is painted or sculpted, is first seen *with the mind's eye*. Well, magic is an art too, and manifestation is definitely an art. So we are now all artists, and we may all look at our goals with our minds' eyes. But we do not force the image, nor do we manipulate it; *we allow it to emerge*. We may be given psychic pictures.

Michelangelo was the master of this process. He created a whole series of sculptures in which he showed how figures can emerge from natural stone. Of course he helped them to emerge; he carved them. But first he saw them with his mind's eye.

Now, let us be aware that just to be able to see a goal, just to allow it to emerge in your mind's eye, is to perceive it. And to perceive it is to create it. If an image is in your mind, and your mind's eye is looking at it, then that image is by definition part of you. If it is part of you, and you allow yourself to identify with it, you have, in effect "become" it. You have created it, and you have manifested it—invisibly. When you understand how this has happened, then the Words of Power that you say to make it manifest visibly and tangibly—the same Words of Power that you may have said before—have subtly changed. They are now working at a different level, because your awareness is at a different level. In other words, your words were attracting before, and now they are creating.

So, the important thing about working at this level is to be aware of how it works. It is not necessary to state Words of Power very differently; you simply state "create" and "manifest" instead of "attract." But it is necessary to think about your words in a different way, to have the idea of creation at the basis of all your work. Also, it is important to keep this idea in mind even when you are not actually working magic. This is not only a different starting point; it is a different reality.

In this new context, here is the way to phase the end of a Words of Power statement:

> . . . I manifest myself as (*state goal*),
> And I create myself as (*state goal*).
> (Always conclude with giving thanks)
> Thank you, Goddess and God,
> And so mote it be.

Now, here is a complete statement:

**Suggested Words of Power for Creation
Manifestation**
There is One Power Which is Goddess and God
Which is Diana, Selene, Hecate, Kernunnos, and Pan
  (*or your other Deities*).
And I (*Your name here*),
Am Diana Incarnate, Selene Incarnate, and Hecate
  Incarnate,
Perfectly aligned with Kemunnos,
  Perfectly aligned with Pan,
I am Witch of Diana, Witch of Selene, Witch of
  Hecate,
Witch of Kernunnos, and Witch of Pan
  I am Priestess of (*fill in alignment*).
My Deities hereby work for and through me,

According to Free Will and for the Good of All
As I hereby manifest and create myself as perfect (*state goal*)
And so mote it be!

Some Guidelines for Creation Manifestation

You may use these Statements for occasions such as self-healing ("I manifest myself as perfect health . . ."), and on occasions when you are actually talking about transforming yourself anyway. But *do not use this Statement when healing another.* I have heard some Witches mistakenly state, "I manifest myself as so-and-so's healing." Instead, with permission you could say, "So and so manifests herself as perfect health."

You may also use the new Statements of self-creation and self-manifestation for calling in a familiar, for work on the holidays, and for Drawing Down the Moon. These Statements may also be used for goals such as the perfect completion of projects or tasks, a material object as meaningful as a home or a tool for work, and any state of being toward which you personally aspire (harmony, love, understanding, wisdom). Remember, of course, that as far as others are involved, as always, manipulation is *out*. Essentially, when in doubt about whether to work in this way, ask your oracles. I suppose the Statements could be used for the goals of just about any material object, but to some people, "I manifest and create myself as a toaster oven" may not feel quite right. (But it is correct.)

I repeat that the important point here is to understand that in effect, you really are creating and manifesting everything in your life in this way, according to the process described previously. Yes, everything, including a toaster oven, should you need one and work for one.

When I first discovered Creation Manifestation, I thought that it was so powerful, and such a paradigm-shift, that it should only be used on special occasions. I now see it as an ongoing method of daily work. How often you use it is up to you.

Group Work

Shared perception, in a group, is a powerful way to create just about anything, whether it's a group of two or a larger group, such as a coven or even an entire community. However, the key word here is "shared." Every participant should hold the same perception, be it a feeling or a mental image. (And it won't work unless it's shared According to Free Will and For the Good of All.)

Remember the basis of the Aspect Theory: This entire lifetime is a perception shared by all its participants. That's what makes this lifetime seem "real" to us. Very often, shared perception in a group is spontaneous and unconscious on the parts of virtually all the group members. Sometimes this shared perception is what links the group together in the first place. Belief can be expressed as an emotion. A negative example of shared perception is a shared fear. Such a shared fear can lend energy (if coming from all the group members) to the feared object. This is important, because deliberate and enlightened group perception can also *solve* a group problem, especially one that has been created in this way. A good example of this is fear of the devil. The entire idea of a devil—as a thought form and as a propagandistic tool—derived all its power from the shared fears of a large group of people. With some people, these shared fears may still be ongoing. If people were to stop fearing the devil, if the idea of a devil were to become completely meaningless to everyone—then the very word "devil" would become a quaint bit of history, alongside other sleazy fictional characters from the past, such as Baal and Beelzebub. Even more important, no one would be moved to act because of the group fear. No one would do anything motivated by belief in the devil—be it voting, attending church, buying a movie ticket, or persecuting a minority.

Think what this idea could mean if people actually stopped fearing the nuclear bomb, or any weapons of mass destruction. I am not suggesting that anyone stop taking this issue seriously, nor deny the potential danger involved, nor stop working for peace. It is a subtle difference. My suggestion is to stop lending such weapons the power of our fear, and then change the ways in which we work against them by purposefully perceiving them as being stripped of all power. This is just one suggestion for group work.

Group work can also be highly effective for changing the World of Form circumstances of the people within the group. Doing group work to help another group, however (such as famine victims in another country), can be more complicated, as this resembles healing work for another person. It is not ethical, or even safe, to say that you manifest and create yourself as another's well being. Also, it is incorrect to say that the others manifest and create themselves, because they may not choose to perceive change in this way.

We can say something like this:

"According to free will and for the good of all, those people have everything they need and want."

However, once we are aware of the process of Creation Manifestation, *everything we work for* automatically uses it, even if you continue to state Words of Power in traditional (Affinity) ways.

The work of Creation Manifestation has a ripple effect. If you go through this doorway, it seems to me that others will follow, and the effects could be far-reaching, to say the least. Just remember that should you choose to work this way in a group, every member of the group should really understand how the technique works. This means that all members of the group should first be able to work this way for themselves.

Lack and Need

These are potentially powerful perceptions, which can get in the way of success in magic. First, let us distinguish between the two. The need is a positive feeling; it is an expression of growth. When you perceive yourself as needing something, that is an acknowledgment of potential fulfillment of the self. Fulfilling a need fulfills the self. Denial of valid needs can create a feeling of lack. "All my needs fulfilled" is a worthwhile goal for Witches or anyone else.

However, this culture sometimes judges valid needs as self-indulgence. In this case, people may deny their needs, and consequently not even try to fulfill them. Or they may feel an urge to overcompensate for needs denied. In either case, if the need is not fulfilled, the person will probably perceive *lack*. Lack is the perception of non-fulfillment and denial. It can create a mood of hopelessness and giving up. Positive Magic provides a means of focusing on our needs and fulfilling them. Creation Manifestation is most effective for perceiving the self as fulfilled and bringing that fulfillment to reality. But what to do about the perception of lack?

When I began this work, the main obstacle that came to my mind was, "What am I supposed to do about the feeling of lack, which definitely is the main problem in Affinity Manifestation?" In other words, how do you prevent that perception of distance from creeping into your awareness, the distance between where you are now and your goal? Such a feeling could really get in the way of really believing that, "I manifest myself and I create myself as—anything." Such a feeling could seriously get in the way of being able to perceive Creation Manifestation as a reality for oneself.

The answer for me was to simply redefine "lack." As what? I define it as a *doorway,* as an opportunity for The Goddess to manifest Herself through your work and through you, and as an idea whose time has come.

Actually, what you're supposed to do is believe so thoroughly and so instantaneously in this work, that spontaneously you just *know* that you have already achieved your goal in Simultaneous Time—because you *know* that linear time is a limited perception, and that the future is really now. Also, you're supposed to know that any feeling of distance is really your own perception, so all you really have to do is let your own perception just get rid of that feeling of distance. Just perceive the space (between having and not having what you need) as closed, as no space, as gone.

I found that most often, this leap of perception was a bit too much for me to handle, especially when I was first learning how to work in this way. I found that I could get to this leap more easily in two steps, rather than one big mental jump. I would just take another look at the distance, the space I might have been perceiving between *having* and *not having*. And I would then redefine that space as a wonderful opportunity. "This space is not lack," I realized, "because calling it lack is really just an effect of negative conditioning from the past."

In this context, lack could actually be seen as a kind of conditioned reflex. The point is to continue beyond that reflex, into choice. So I would definitely *acknowledge* the feeling of lack (of course, not deny it), and then consciously choose to *redefine* it—as a doorway for The Goddess to come through into my life. Instead of lack, it became an opportunity for Her work to manifest through me. Some good steps for accomplishing this are:

> The Goddess created me;
> I perceived (created) a lack;
> Taking responsibility for doing this (with no guilt or
> blame of course),
> I now choose to create a solution;
> As I am Goddess incarnate
> I now allow The Goddess to manifest the solution
> through me.

Therefore, instead of a negative idea (lack), you now have a positive idea (opportunity). "There must be a good reason for this opportunity," I would realize. Even in terms of linear time perception, this works! The reason for this opportunity is that it's time for whatever the solution is, to manifest. The opportunity is an idea whose time has come! Thus, through your perception, you transform *lack* into *an idea whose time has come.*

So, when you get to the point of knowing that it's time for you to work for something, and if you wish to work with Creation Manifestation, first be aware that you are now at a crossroads. Here you can choose between perceiving yourself to be in lack, or perceiving yourself as an embodiment of an idea whose time has come. Your situation can be a doorway for The Goddess to come through. All you have to do is allow yourself to see it that way.

The Crossroads is Hecate's domain, and Hecate rules choices. So a wonderful way to begin would be to call on Hecate to help you with this process.

When you make a choice, you transform yourself. You are transformed from who you were before you made that choice into who you are now that you have made the choice. In this case the choice is to manifest your work in this way: to create yourself and to manifest yourself as your goal.

When you create yourself and manifest yourself as your goal, you are also transformed. You are transformed into a new version of yourself; you become yourself plus the embodiment of your goal. You are yourself, and you are also your goal. **You Are Your Goal!**

As Yeats put it:

"O body swayed to music, O brightening glance,
How can we know the dancer from the dance?"[5]

We cannot tell the dancer from the dance, and should not expect to; because when the dancer becomes the dance, the dancer *is* the dance. That's the whole idea!

You are your goal.

You are the transformation that embodies your goal.

You are the transformation. Magic is transformation.

You are the magic.

part three

Afterword

CHAPTER 16

Morphogenetic Fields

Just in time for the Millennium, and for the accompanying spread of magical practice and spirituality, came the fascinating new development in the science of quantum physics. This field echoes many Witchcraft and occult techniques. Here are some examples: The hypothesis that cause and effect can be reversed, and the axiom that the observer affects the observed—and my favorite, morphogenetic fields as described by Rupert Sheldrake.[1]

Put very simply, a morphogenetic or morphic field is a live force field formed around every living thing, which has regenerative and duplicating properties. It imbues other living beings with abilities to duplicate behavior, and even to replicate the physical form of the original being sending out the field. This can be seen to explain everything from evolution to ESP, as well as countless previously unexplainable phenomena. I do not mean to suggest that Rupert Sheldrake has related his hypothesis in any way to the processes of magic. But for our purposes here, the theory can be extrapolated to apply to the transformative work of Positive Magic and The Witches' Threefold Law. Performing an act of magic can be seen as creating a force field, which extends through time and space to create the planned effect. And according to this theory, the continuous practice of magic according to "For the Good of All" can be seen as increasing the numbers of individuals and groups who work in this way. And this eventually affects the nature of so-called "reality." If enough people believe that perception creates reality, and enough people proceed to work magic to create their own realities in a directed and ethical manner, then more and more people will do this. And the process will be repeated until it redefines the way reality is dealt with, *en masse,* in our world.

As in days of old, it starts with the Witches.

CHAPTER 17

The Role and the True Self

Just when I thought my personal theology was complete, I had a major discovery that has influenced all of my work, and upon which I have based workshops and audiotapes. This has made me aware that any worthwhile theology—personal, traditional, Witchcraft, or otherwise—is always in process and in progress.

The Role

Questions: What do you do if all of your magical work manifests according to plan—except for several specific areas? What does it mean if you realize, on closest scrutiny, that you must still have some negative resignation lurking in your psyche—because there seem to be some areas where *you don't even expect* your magic to work? Do you secretly believe that there are some areas of life where compromise, or even denial, might actually be *necessary?* How do you reconcile the above three questions with your Positive Witchcraft belief in the Infinity of

Solution, which posits a potential solution for *everything*, albeit in essence, and in the appropriate form?

Answer: Maybe you have not been practicing Witchcraft from your *True Self* all along, at least not consistently. Maybe some of the time, you have been working out of a part of yourself that is known in popular family psychology parlance as your *role* (role identity). Usually, this role has been determined by society, by early childhood conditioning and family dynamics. I prefer to call it *the* role, rather than *your* (or *my* role), because I feel it is best not to "own" a problem or difficulty. I believe that the first step toward releasing a problem is to disown it and not claim it any longer as yours. This is in the same spirit as when we do a healing; we never say, "my," "his," or "her" illness. We say "the" illness.

Because family roles are integral to our society, and have been for centuries, they have gone relatively unexplored and even unnoticed, until quite recently. Consequently, at this time, virtually everyone in our culture has experienced a family role. Typical roles are: leader, martyr, jester, scapegoat, savior, helper, and victim. The role represents a limited perception of the Self, which can permeate all of life and ultimately determine our worldview. Although a role can be a residual effect of another life, most roles are usually assigned and defined throughout childhood. Later, during adulthood, one can modify it, or—with deep work and conviction—actually release the role and locate the True Self. Or one could remain stuck in the role for one's whole life, with complete lack of awareness and total denial. Then, one could consequently reenact the role's script over and over again with different people, including spouses, employers, children, and strangers. I must emphasize that there is absolutely no blame in living out a role, because the original function of role is literally a lifesaver. Early in life, accepting the role assigned to one is often the child's sole means of adaptation and survival. But the role outlives its usefulness in personal development, in adulthood.

Stated in Positive Witchcraft terms, the role usually bypasses much use of Personal Power and conscious connection to the Divine. Most people begin to shed roles and search for their True Selves during adolescence. Most thoughtful people, with work, effort, therapy, religion, and other self-help programs, manage to locate their True Selves and live out of their True Selves most of the time. But most people do not succeed in locating their True Selves *all* of the time—because they cannot really tell when they are living out of the role.

To put it as briefly as possible, for purposes of this chapter:

For non-Witches, the role usually manifests in areas of life where people feel that compromise is unavoidable. Roles can also manifest as disease, both mental and physical, as the True Self literally cries out for healing and expresses itself in tangible metaphors. The role is often expressed in a whole litany of personal problems, including phobias, addictions, controlling behavior, and depression.

For Witches, the role can manifest in these same problems—but also in the added area of *limiting magical practice*. The role identity may believe that these are some situations in which magic simply does not work. In these situations, the practice of magic may be blocked by negative resignation, denial, or failure, and might actually appear to exist somehow outside of the Infinity of Solution. Of course, this is illusion.

Your True Self

At the risk of sounding simplistic, the best antidotes for Witches and non-Witches alike are:

1. To first achieve awareness of the problem (or actually, the challenge), as an existing role.

2. To release the role and access the True Self. The True Self is the microcosmic connection to the macrocosm, and that connection would feel good in any religion, or even in a non-religion or philosophy. The True Self is plugged directly into the infinite Universal Power. In practical Witchcraft terms, this includes the conscious use of the Infinity of Solution. In effect, one calls upon and uses one's True Self to release the role.

There are a number of ways to accomplish this. In my workshops, we work with Homer's *Odyssey*, and do various exercises to locate the feelings of both True Self and role. For some people, these forays into self-awareness provide sufficient means to access the True Self and to be ready to keep on tracking it from that point on, and to avoid the role. For myself, I needed a major ritual. I also needed to share the ritual in the ancient Witchcraft communal way. The simple ritual I originally chose is this: First, Words of Power are used to release the Roles and replace them with our True Selves.

With the one Power working for me and through me,
I hereby release this role and the role that has been in
    my life, which it represents

And I replace the role with my True Self
And so mote it be.

Then every participant takes a roll—yes, a bakery type of roll—and each person tears that up into little pieces. The pieces are later fed to the birds, thereby transformed literally *for the good of all*. Then everyone in the workshop pounds a drum or other noisemaker, and we rhythmically chant, "My True Self!" over and over, all together, until a feeling of joy comes over us.

From then on, "*My True Self!*" serves as a mantra for daily life.

We also have further developments detailing the facets of the role and the True Self, with symptoms to be watched for, and verbal and visual "antidotes" to be applied. These are all helpful *forms*, which serve to keep us watchful. I have also identified and developed a new concept—The True Self permeating all of life. Needing a name for it, I dubbed it my *New Paradigm*, which represents the projection of the True Self into every area of life, including the future. And this idea is expressed in the chants and mantras, too. Here is a simple mantra, which I find most helpful for remembering: "*My True Self, My New Paradigm!*"

I repeat this throughout the day, if I feel I need it. The basic healing fact is that perception of the role as reality, is transformed into perception of the True Self as reality. This, the True Self reality is a wonderful foundation for a fulfilling life.

This is the case for anyone, but here it applies specifically to Positive Witchcraft work.[1] Meanwhile, to use this concept in your Words of Power work, you may add this focus to the end of all your Words of Power Statements:

"... From My True Self
To My True Self."
(And So Mote It Be.)

CHAPTER 18

Ethics, Choices, and the "W" Word

Now that Witchcraft has returned in such a meaningful way to our planet, and now that we have committed ourselves to living full time as Witches, we know that, for those of us fortunate enough to be living in areas of religious freedom, such as the United States, we actually have laws to protect us as we practice our religion. We truly believe that Positive Witchcraft and Positive Magic can help our planet, and we are renewed in our age-old Witches' sense of responsibility to help the community, including our global village. Now—whom do we tell? And when? And why? The goal, of course, is to be able to tell everybody, to live openly as Witches, and to help our culture understand that ours is as acceptable as any mainstream belief system. But how to get there?

Because I have been dealing with this issue for more than thirty years, I can provide some practical guidelines. At this moment in time, circumstances are enormously better for Witches than they have been in centuries. Nonetheless, we can say that some problems still exist for Witches, depending on the neighborhood and the social arena. Therefore, we may conclude that *discretion is still the better part of valor.*

Witchcraft as a Minority Religion

In some places there may be outright persecution, not only of Witches, but of any minority religious groups. In some social situations, simply being a Witch can be used against one, especially when people are looking for any excuse to cause problems. I have seen distressing items in the news about Witchcraft being used as an issue in custody battles. Sometimes parents and spouses misunderstand our motives for embracing our religion, and I know instances of Witchcraft being used as a reason for people having been fired from their jobs. I have encountered serious bias in workplaces over the years myself. I have experienced problems in radio and television, and certain bookstores have refused to carry my books because the titles have included the words "Witchcraft" and "Occult."

In addition to the more serious problems of discrimination, is a pervasive attitude of denigration and trivialization that some people still carry, assuming that Witchcraft is some kind of joke. How many of us have been asked to turn people into frogs or "put a spell" on someone, or something else totally ridiculous?

One of the problems seems to be that most people still don't know what Witches really are. Even now, Witches seem to be considered either in league with the devil, or totally fictitious. Many older, incorrect definitions in dictionaries and encyclopedias still reflect this. Even folklore and fairy tales with "Wicked Witches" causing harm, have not yet all been cleansed into political correctness. All of these factors can perpetuate misunderstandings. This, of course, is a major motivation for "coming out" in the first place—to clear the air, to clarify and redefine our Craft. That is certainly the main reason I made my practice of Witchcraft more public than most.

But when does the act of coming out become foolhardy and counterproductive, and when is it the karmically correct thing to do? Only each one of us can know for ourselves, and each circumstance is different.

Out of the Broom Closet

Why do you want to come out? Remember that telling people you are a Witch has an effect. It can be sensational or scandalous, it can be misunderstood, it can get in the way of clear communication with others. It can create martyrdom, even in a relatively mild social sense, or create more serious problems. Or it can enlighten people, and pave the way for future Witches.

Remember, being a Witch is nothing to be ashamed of, but it is nothing to boast about either.

Most Witches carry complex karma from other lives, and this often can include the issues of persecution, and emotional reasons for either hiding or living openly as a Witch. I believe that even more important than saying you're a Witch is *living consistently as a Positive Witch* (even in private):

+ Helping others for the good of all.

+ Honoring the environment.

+ Living by Positive Magic and Positive Witchcraft on a daily basis.

+ Always maintaining a holistic attitude toward religion This means, incidentally, not insulting other religions. Too often I have heard Witches denigrating Judaism or Christianity without realizing the difficult karma that this can create. Witchcraft is holistic and right-brained. This means that the Witch's beliefs do not preclude the validity of other belief systems.

+ Helping the community connect to the Invisible, and helping others to rediscover the power and the use of Positive Magic.

In other words, being a Witch does not depend on *saying* that you're a Witch. It depends on how you live your life.

When in doubt about telling people, consult your oracles. At this time, my personal policy is this: I am totally up front and honest about Witchcraft in my work, and among my friends and associates. But I usually don't mention it in areas where it truly does not apply and would only be a distraction. (For example, when buying groceries.) If your identity as a Witch is not even remotely a part of the picture, there's simply no reason to bring it up—just as most people don't usually announce at all times, in every circumstance, what their traditional religion is. I have asked my friends to please not reveal to others what my religion is, because I prefer to keep it private when I'm not working—unless, of course, it is somehow relevant.

Often people ask me what my pentagram means, because I wear my Witchcraft jewelry quite openly. I usually ask, "Do you know what this means?" If they say, "Yes," that's fine with me. If they say, "No," or ask me what it means, I simply say, "This is magical," or "This means good luck," and then I drop the subject. I once walked into a store, and the saleswoman noticed my pentagram and delivered a tirade on its negative meaning. I really didn't have time for a debate. So sometimes (ouch!) I tuck it under my collar. It all depends where I am. If people I don't know recognize me because of my work, and want to discuss Witchcraft, I generally give them the short version: "Witchcraft is a religion and a philosophy. No, of course we don't worship a devil; we worship The Goddess. It's an ancient nature religion." And this is also where the politically correct "Wicca" comes in, if necessary. I have found that the main function of the word "Wicca" is that it deflects the negative connotation most people have with Witchcraft, simply because most mainstream people have never heard "Wicca" before. When getting to know someone really well, naturally, a longer version of explaining Witchcraft and what it means to us is part of being one's True Self and being honest. But that does not mean to proselytize or try to convert people. Our explanation should always be neutral in nature. Witches do not proselytize, because we believe in equal Power. Also we respect, on the deepest level, everyone's right to choose his or her own religious beliefs. Our reality is not threatened by anyone else's worldview. Our reality *includes* the possibility for everyone else's reality to be true (for them), too.

As Positive Witches, we earn the right to be open Witches by staying responsible and ethical Witches; this creates the foundation for Witchcraft's reemergence in the world. The responsible practice of Positive Witchcraft itself, and the ensuing focus on this, will create its own appropriate atmosphere. I believe blanket openness will inevitably follow. Remember the principle of morphogenetic fields.

Ethics

It is important to ask ourselves, "Why have I chosen to be a Witch?" and to face the answers honestly. Let us admit that for many of us, Pagan beliefs in general, and Witchcraft beliefs in particular, contain a healthy respite from Judeo-Christian definitions of morality. We have no authority figures to direct or watch over us, or to threaten us with hellfire or a Deity's wrath, in order to keep us in line. But let us also remember that our beliefs contain their own morality.

The Judeo-Christian code of ethics has served a worthwhile function, notwithstanding its undeniable abuses. Some parts of this code may even have originated with Pagan beliefs. For example, "Do unto others as you would have them do unto you," is totally Pagan in spirit. People who truly follow the Judeo-Christian code with commitment in their hearts are among the most ethical and spiritual people on our planet. As Witches, I believe that we must acknowledge and honor this. In absence of such a code, the beliefs of Witchcraft do not mean carte blanche for irresponsible behavior in any area of life. This misconception provided horrible propaganda to fuel the fires of the persecutions in the Middle Ages and early New England Witchhunts. In a repressive society, open sexuality has always been considered the devil's work. Regrettably, however rarely, I have seen our religion used as an excuse for such divergent behaviors as: polygamy, group sex, civil disobedience, and drug use (not that

I am condemning these behaviors here—it's just that none of them is even remotely related to the religion of Witchcraft). All this is mentioned before we even get to the inevitable discussion of unethical magic.

Left Brain/Right Brain

I recently found out that I have been called "The Ethics Witch." That's a nice title—but why? Here is what I think: Witchcraft is inherently one of the most ethical endeavors a human being can enter into—if one practices it in a vacuum. Far from a life of isolation, we are now in the 21st century. Specifically, we are currently emerging from a culture of so-called *rational* thought into an age of *holistic* thought. We are moving away from a left-brained society, in which polarizing ideologies and positions have been accepted as the norm. It had actually become a given circumstance, accepted as "reality" to believe that in order to get ahead one must first see that other people are not successful. In this context, success has been measured in terms of other people's failure, and rivalry is considered good sport. We are now leaving this frame of reference and moving into a right-brained culture, in which we know we are very much all together on this planet—in which tolerance is becoming widespread, and in which differences are no longer threatening but embraced within the larger whole. Today, the belief that *we are all linked* is no longer limited to Witchcraft, and is becoming part of everyone's daily life. The concept that *everyone can be a winner* is beginning to become a viable reality, at least potentially.

However, as our world experiences this transition, let us admit that we Witches might still be influenced by the culture into which we were born. How could we not be? So we must be vigilant. We must be vigilant not only because people are watching us (which they are), but because magic is a potentially powerful tool for harm. People who do not practice magic might openly create harm for others by their actions, because they think, mistakenly, that this is the only way to succeed at something. But for Witches, the potential for harming others is even greater, because creating harm through the use of magic can cause a more hidden, and yet more dramatic and terrible result.

Unethical Magic

We all know that magic should never be used for harm, but sometimes this misuse can come about even without our conscious awareness. This can happen in two possible circumstances, both involved with insufficient commitment to Positive Witchcraft:

1. Magic can be misused if we do not believe in our religion deeply enough to practice it consistently. If a Witch doubts her/his foundation—the power of magic—or takes it too lightly, this could lead to manipulative magic. This can occur most often in a competitive situation. It could be a team event, an election, or any area in which a specific outcome is desired. Remember, we never work magic to "win!" In fact, we champion the concept that the ideal solution is always everybody wins. That's the right-brain concept, using the Infinity of Solution. Manipulation is always

manipulation, and it's always unnecessary, because for the good of all is always just that—for the good of all! Every magical act is a serious one, with serious consequences.

2. Another possible misuse of magic without conscious awareness could come about if a Witch doubts her or his own Personal Power. Here we can get into a murky area of dealing with criminals or actual evildoers. Some Witches believe that it's appropriate to try to "stop" such people from committing harmful acts. This is not the correct focus in order to achieve the effects we want, which are safety and protection. Most of the time, in such cases, the most powerful result comes from using your magic for helping the police and other appropriate agencies, also for protecting all who are involved. Focus on protection—on protecting yourself, and if necessary, directing your protection to cover all victims or even potential victims according to Free Will and For The Good of All. Trust in your power to accomplish this effectively.

I have heard that some Witches believe it is somehow necessary to "punish" perpetrators of crimes, or to wreak revenge. I truly understand the impulse, but there are no exceptions to the rule of creating karma. Trust in The Threefold Law (or your own version of the Law of Return) enough to let *it* take care of any perpetrator.

Remember, magic should never be doubted nor taken lightly. This means never doubt your Personal Power to the extent that you might harm another by mistakenly thinking it's somehow the correct or necessary thing to do.

In all circumstances, let us return to the basic foundation of our religion by always remembering our fundamental tenet:

Remember the Threefold Law
If you believe that perception creates reality—
And that perceiving The Threefold Law makes it
    real—
Then The Threefold Law is as real as the magic upon
    which it is based.
We work our magic here, in the Visible World, the
    World of Form;
It goes out into the Invisible World,
And returns to us in the World of Form.
Everything you do always comes back to you.
This is how magic works.
So this is the way that intention returns to the sender,
    as well as sendee, or recipient.
You don't have to work at being ethical;
It is built into the magic, automatically.
It is for the good of all.

Notwithstanding a recent trend by a small group of original-thinking Witches (to veer away from accepting the traditional Threefold Law), I still believe that this Law serves our religion as well today as in ages past. I also consider it a profound metaphor for the Positive Magic process.

By means of morphogenetic fields, every action of practicing helpful magic expands the circle of help to ever-greater numbers. By means of morphogenetic fields, Positive Witchcraft presents a model of correct magical endeavor for the rest of the world.

Whenever a feeling is voiced with truth and frankness,
Whenever a deed is a clear expression of sentiment,
A mysterious and far-reaching influence is exerted.
At first it acts on those who are inwardly receptive.
But the circle grows larger and larger.
The root of all influence lies in one's inner being:
Given true and vigorous expression in word and deed
    its effect is great.

> —*The I Ching*
> Hexagram 61
> Nine in the second place

CHAPTER 19

Serving the Community

Even though we use our magic to enrich our own lives and those of our loved ones, let us remember that the ancient role of Witch was to help the community. Now we can retranslate this role into modern times. We may still bless crops, fields, woods, seas, animals, and plant life. We may still bless the health of people of all ages, both born and unborn. But let us also address our work as it applies to modern needs: To purify the Earth, Air, Fire, and Water of our planet. Let us send light and protection, peace, nourishment, and understanding to individuals and groups that need it, according to free will and for the good of all, only. Let us remember the Macrocosm at all times, and our integral connection—as microcosms—to every living being.

Some Goals

Some of our goals are to find out why we were born into this lifetime, this planet, and this culture—and to fulfill that discovery.

+ To understand why we have chosen to be Witches, and to fulfill that choice.

+ To live fully as Positive Witches, according to our beliefs.

+ To believe and to prove to ourselves—and to prove to others by our living example—that there is nothing and no one to fear.

+ To clear the name of Witchcraft; to spread the information about Positive Magic, so that a world that has forgotten may benefit from it once again.

+ To work our Positive Witches' magic for unequivocal peace and safety on our home planet.

+ To perfect Earth Magic, that it may extend beyond the planet Earth.

My Personal Words of Power for the 21st Century

(This statement is for women; men can make the appropriate Alignment adjustments. Both women and men can fill in any Deity Alignments of choice.)

> Now I go into the castle,
> And here I decree and proclaim
> That there is One Power Which is Goddess and God
> Which includes Diana, Hecate, Selene, Kernunnos,
>   Pan, Ceres, Neptune, Isis, Osiris, Horus, and
>   Ceridwenn.

And I, (*Witch's name*), am Goddess Incarnate.
   I am Witch of Diana, Witch of Selene, Witch of
   Hecate, Witch of Kernunnos, Witch of Pan, Witch
   of Ceres, Witch of Neptune, Witch of Isis, Witch of
   Osiris, Witch of Horus, Witch of Ceridwenn.
I am Diana incarnate, Selene incarnate, Hecate Incar-
   nate
Perfectly Aligned with Kernunnos, perfectly with Pan
I am Ceres Incarnate, perfectly Aligned with Neptune
I am Isis Incarnate, perfectly Aligned with Osiris, per-
   fectly Aligned with Horus.
I am Ceridwenn Incarnate.
I am Priestess of Diana.
I hereby create and manifest this book and all that's
   in it
As divine perfection,
To go out into the world in safety, protection, and joy
For the good of all and according to free will,
To help myriad beings,
To cleanse the name of Witchcraft into its correct
   identity as positive and life-affirming,
To help all Witches, and to help our planet Earth
And beyond,
As we move peacefully, safely, and successfully into the
   21st Century
And beyond,
From my True Self,
And so mote it be!

CHAPTER NOTES

Chapter 2

1. Some modern Witches have chosen not to follow this belief, further proving that Witchcraft is definitely not an organized religion.
2. For further details, see *Positive Magic: A Toolkit for the Modern Witch.* Marion Weinstein, Chapter 8. Weiser Books, MA 2020. Also refer to Marion Weinstein's audiotape, *How to Use Words of Power.* Earth Magic Productions.

Chapter 8

1. You may use the longer form, using all your Alignments.

Chapter 9

1. For more on this subject, see "Reincarnation in Pets and Familiars," by Marion Weinstein, an article originally published in *Of A Like Mind.*
2. There is a wonderful new field, called Animal Communication, which extends the benefits of interspecies communication, including with the Spirit World—to any animal lover. For more information see *www.animaltalk.net.*

Chapter 10

1. James Von Praagh has several excellent books, including *Talking To Heaven, A Medium's Message of Life After Death*, E. P. Dutton, NY, 1997. Also see Marianne Michaels, *A Second Chance to Say Goodbye*, written with Anita Curtis. Infinity Publishing, PA 2002.

Chapter 11

1. These theories appear in *The Morning of The Magicians*. Jacques Bergier and Louis Pauwels, NY, Dover Books.

Chapter 12

1. The use of the word "manifest" in this ritual will be explained fully in part two, which follows.

Chapter 13

1. The body of work by the late Jane Roberts and her channeled entity, Seth, provides the best material I have yet found on this subject. In fact, most information in this section of Earth Magic has been greatly influenced by one of her books, *Adventures in Consciousness*, which is highly recommended.
2. Jane Roberts calls this the "Oversoul," which is considered the highest and most developed form of the self.

Chapter 15

1. See Chapter One of *Positive Magic*, by the author, for amplification of this idea.
2. This is not meant as a "put-down" of any religion or prayer. In fact, I have been careful to cite just a fragment of a typical Western religious prayer (considered "non-denominational") in English.
3. The best book I have ever read on this subject is *The Laws of Manifestation*, by David Spangler. Published by Findhorn Publications, Scotland, this book was an important influence and source of inspiration for this chapter. However, in this book, as well as on the back cover, David Spangler states unequivocally, "Manifestation is not magic." According to Free Will, this is absolutely true for him and for those who wish to embrace his frame of reference. However,

this does not diminish the importance of his book in my research or other areas of my work.

4. The exception here, I believe, is the hereditary Witch. In families of practicing Witches, the Creation method could be taught to children as part of family tradition, because such children would not be burdened by contradictory cultural perceptions that adult "converts" to Witchcraft seem to have.

5. Among School Children. From *The Collected Poems of W. B. Yeats.* New York: The MacMillian Company, 1956.

Chapter 16

1. This work can be found in *A New Science of Life, The Hypothesis of Causative Formation,* by Rupert Sheldrake, Jeremy P. Tarcher, Inc., Los Angeles, 1981.

Chapter 17

1. For further details on this, see the audiotape *Personal Magic, The Role and the True Self,* Earth Magic Productions, N.Y., 1997.

BIBLIOGRAPHY

Adler, Margot. *Drawing Down The Moon: Pagans, Druids and Goddess Worshippers in America Today,* New York: Viking Press, 1981.

Bergier, Jacques and Louis Pauwels. *The Morning of The Magicians,* New York: Dover Books, 1968.

Bradshaw, John. *On The Family, A Revolutionary Way of Self-Discovery.* Boca Raton, FL: Health Communications, Inc., 1988.

Cameron, Julia, with Mark Bryan. *The Artist's Way: A Spiritual Path to Higher Creativit.,* New York, NY: A Jeremy P. Tarcher/Putnam Book, published by G.P. Putnam's Sons, 1992.

Dewr, Dagonet, ed. *New Witch Magazine,* Indiana, Quarterly.

Drew, A. J. *Wicca for Couples.* Franklin Lakes, NJ: New Page Books, 2002.

—— *Wicca for Men.* Franklin Lakes, NJ: New Page Books, 2002.

Fox, Selena, ed. *The Circle Guide to Pagan Groups: Nature Spirituality Networking Source Book,* Circle, Wisconsin, annually.

—— *Circle Magazine,* Nature Spirituality Quarterly, Circle, Wisconsin.

Grabhorn, Lynn. *Excuse Me, Your Life is Waiting, The Astonishing Power of Feelings.* Charlottesville, VA: Hampton Roads Publishing Inc., 2000.

Guiley, Rosemary Ellen. *The Encyclopedia of Witches and Witchcraft.* Second Edition, Checkmark Books, New York: 1999.

Henes, Donna. *Celestially Auspicious Occasions: Seasons, Cycles, and Celebrations,* New York: Perigee: Putnam/Berkley, 1996.

King, Viki. *Beyond Visualization: Feel It In Your Heart, Have It In Your Life,* Novato, CA: New World Library, 1992.

Michaels, Marianne, with Anita Curtis. *A Second Chance To Say Goodbye.* Conshohocken, PA: Infinity Publishing, 2002.

Nightmare, M. Macha. *Witchcraft and The Web,* Toronto: ECW Press, 2001.

Roberts, Jane. *Adventures in Consciousness,* New York: Bantam 1979.

Sheldrake, Rupert. *A New Science of Life, The Hypothesis of Formative Causation.* Los Angeles: Jeremy P. Tarcher, Inc., 1981.

Spangler, David. *The Laws of Manifestation,* Findhorn, Moray, Scotland: Findhorn Publications, 1983.

Stone, Merlin. *Ancient Mirrors of Womanhood,* Boston: Beacon, 1979, third printing 1991.

Valiente, Doreen. *An ABC of Witchcraft Past and Present,* New York: Saint Martin's Press, 1973.

—— *Where Witchcraft Lives,* Cedar Knolls, NJ: Wehman, 1962.

—— *Witchcraft For Tomorrow,* New York: St. Martin's Press, 1978.

Von Praagh, James. *Talking to Heaven, A Medium's Message of Life After Death.* New York: E. P. Dutton, 1997.

Walker, Barbara G. *The Woman's Dictionary of Symbols and Sacred Objects.* San Francisco: Harper & Row 1988.

Weinstein, Marion. *Positive Magic, Ancient Metaphysical Techniques For Modern Lives,* Revised Edition, Franklin Lakes, NJ: New Page Books, 2002.

Willhelm, Richard. Trans. (German) *The I Ching or Book of Changes,* trans. (English) by Cary F. Baynes, Princeton, NJ: Bollingen Series XIX, Princeton University Press, 1983.

Yeats, William Butler, *The Collected Poems of W. B. Yeats,* New York: The MacMillan Company, 1966.

Websites

These represent just a few of the many excellent related websites.
The Covenant of The Goddess: *www.cog.org.*
Rupert Sheldrake: *www.sheldrake.org.*
Circle Sanctuary: *www.circlesanctuary.org.*

Permissions

Selena Fox, one of the most amazing Wiccan Priestesses on this planet, provided the information for the following sections: The Witch's Bottle and The Four Directions in the Morning Ritual.

The information for the section on Feel-o-vision was inspired by two books:

Viki King's *Beyond Visualization: Feel It in Your Heart, Have It In Your Life* (New World Library) and Lynn Grabhorn's *Excuse Me, Your Life Is Waiting: The Astonishing Power of Feelings.* (Hampton Roads Publishing Company, Inc.)

Selections quoted from *The I Ching* or *Book of Changes.* The Richard Wilhelm translation, rendered into English by Carey F. Baynes, Bollingen series XIX, Princeton University Press.

ABOUT THE AUTHOR

Marion Weinstein (1939–2009) was an author, teacher, media personality, and proud New York "city witch." Known as "The Ethics Witch" she is one of the founders of the modern Witchcraft movement. She was the first to coin the phrase and define Positive Magic, and clearly delineate its use. Her radio show, "Marion's Cauldron," was the first regularly scheduled Wiccan and psychic programming on record, and was a New York phenomena for fourteen years. Her first book, *Positive Magic,* was first published in 1978 and soon became a beloved classic.

TO OUR READERS